Alice

In

GenderLand

One wife's journey
with her transgendered husband

By Heidi Hansen

i

ii

Alice
In
GenderLand

ISBN: 978—0998252681

Published by H3Press,
         PO Box 312, Carlsborg, WA 98324

Dedication

To my family and friends who supported me through this journey, and to all those who will venture this path. This is not an isolated incident and more common now than then. I offer it as a point of discussion for others who contemplate crossing gender lines and those who love them.

Table of Contents

Author's Notes

A note about the use of pronouns: When referring to Martin pre-operative, he and him are used; post-operative, she and her are used for Maureen.

"Be Curious,
Not Judgmental"

Ted Lasso

Prologue

The Queen of Hearts was chasing Alice when I woke. Two of my sons were stretched out on the sofa on either side of me, asleep. I clicked off the TV and carried them to bed.

When I slipped into the master bedroom, my husband lay sprawled on the bed, peering into his laptop, the TV blaring across the room. At the sound of the door shutting behind me, he snapped the laptop shut and scurried into the bathroom. Passing through the bathroom to the walk-in closet, I caught his reflection in the mirror. Something was wrong. I blinked, then blinked again. What was I seeing?

"What?" I stammered. "What are you doing?"

He quickly bent over the sink, splashing water on his face. The lipstick and rouge smeared; the mascara ran down his cheeks. Our eyes met for a second in the mirror.

He grabbed a towel and ducked into the shower. I stood staring at my reflection.

What had I witnessed?

What did it mean?

I Am Alice

I think of myself as Alice. Alice with her blonde hair and blue eyes epitomized innocence. I was as innocent as Alice. When Martin said he wanted to dress up in women's clothes, I was horrified. I felt as if I fell down the rabbit hole into a topsy-turvy world where nonsense was the norm.

After that first blurt out and my reaction of tears, we skirted the issue.

Following his skirmish with cancer several years later, he said, "I have had to face my death, I can't put off what I have to do."

I waited for what it was he had to do. I was clueless. Was it to put on a dress? Wear makeup in the privacy of our bedroom? Or something more?

The steps were tiny. Did he purposely go slow for me? I wondered what it was that he alluded to in his retelling of an EST-like weekend where he said he had been backed into a corner and said something that he wished he could take back. He would never tell me what that was. I would never have guessed that he said that he wanted to be a woman.

"Look in the mirror!" I wanted to shout. "How can you be a woman?" Everything I knew about being a woman did not fit with what I saw. He was huge – six feet tall, over two hundred fifty pounds, muscular legs, barrel chest, beefy arms. Additionally, he had a heavy dark beard, a prominent brow ridge, and a deep voice. How could you carve a woman from that?

"Look at how you dress," I said. "You wear the same pants every day, the black cotton socks, the athletic shoes, the short sleeve polyester shirts. Where is your sense of style? You shave, comb your hair and go. You don't wash your face; you never brush your teeth except at bedtime."

"I will when I am a woman," he said.

But I am getting ahead of myself. It would take another ten years before he would blurt out in counseling that he wanted to be a woman.

Back at the beginning, he asked me to put makeup on him. He wanted to know how it felt. I reluctantly agreed. I applied foundation, blush and lipstick. He closed his eyes, and I drew eyeliner across his eyelids, brushed on eye shadow and mascara., and sat back to see how it looked. Could I have been wrong? Did I see a woman there? He pulled me to him and kissed me.

I pushed back, rose and hurried across the room. He had gone too far. There was a taint of perversion that was unpalatable to me. Down the rabbit hole, where nothing is what it seems or should be. I am in my house, my children are in their rooms, but this person is no longer my partner, my trusted ally. Who is he?

I wrote these pages using fictional names for some. An effort to give us space and privacy. But as I edit and replace the fictional names, I come face to face with a problem. I am no longer the person I wrote about. I am both embarrassed and pitying the character I express here as Alice. I want to slap her, snap her back to reality. Why does she persist in waiting for the inevitable? Why does she remain quiet?

At the same time, I can step back into that time and recall my motivation. I wanted to hold fast to the life we had. I wanted to maintain the life that our children were accustomed to. I knew that divorce would mean giving up the house, letting go of half.

I felt it unfair. How could all this be because of his thought that he should be a woman? How could I sustain my life and that for our four sons?

Once Upon a Time

I was like that girl in the wonderland stories. We both had blonde hair and blue eyes. The similarities extended to an extraordinary innocence and naivety. I did not think that of myself then, but as I look back, I am dismayed to see how narrow my expectations were.

To share my journey, I must travel back, all the way back, to the beginning. My memories of our start are faded and stained by what came next. There was once a fairy tale quality to our lives.

Pulling the photo album off the shelf, I opened it and flipped through the pages. At the beginning was a photo of Martin and me in the blush of new love. Martin stood tall and proud, chest out, head high. I gleamed with happiness. The photo was taken at the company holiday party; I wore an off-the-shoulder black dress with rhinestone buttons. That dress was sophisticated and classy. Martin's brown hair fell in soft curls covering his ears and shirt collar; his eyes sparkled with promise. He wore a dark gray suit and together we danced, at one point, breaking into a polka around the dance floor to the delight of our peers. It was a magical night.

We felt we found in each other what was missing in our lives. We were ready to stop looking further, we wanted to build our family and snuggle in.

As I turned the pages, our life together replayed.

Our early conversations were about what mattered to us and what we wanted. We both wanted a fulfilling family life. He wanted children. I already had a two-year-old son.

My parents were about to celebrate their fortieth wedding anniversary, and I had a family of six sisters.

At twenty-one, I married my high school sweetheart, but the marriage faltered when I wanted a family, and he chose the single life. The pain of a failed marriage and divorce left me feeling unloved, unwanted, and discarded. I knew I had a lot to offer but attempts at dating failed to produce the desired results. I was far from miserable. I had my adorable and bright two-year-old son, Henry. I loved my job. I was the first woman manager in a high-tech company and a respected member of the management team.

I lived near my parents and saw my sisters often. They were my support team watching my son when I needed help.

Meeting Martin was like a dream come true. He was everything I wanted in a husband: he was intelligent, well-educated, fun to be with, and our values seemed to mesh. He had been raised Jewish but was not practicing. When Christmas time rolled around, he fell in love with my whole family and was as excited as a kid to hand out presents from beneath the tree. Of course, coming from a small family, my big family could overwhelm, but he seemed to love it all; my parents, my sisters, the brothers-in-law, nieces and nephews.

I longed for a partner who would share in the joy of watching my son grow into adulthood, maybe another child. One of the hardest parts of being a single parent is not having someone to share your child's development.

"He cut his first tooth."

"He took his first step."

"He can count to twenty."

Most of all, I wanted a partner for the rest of my life, not just for a season. I wanted the happily ever after ending.

When Martin was finishing high school, his parents divorced leaving him with an angry mother and a confused younger brother. His mother wasn't prepared to support the household alone and soon invited her parents to move in. All this made for the total disintegration of what Martin had come to believe was his perfect life.

Martin had been in a couple of long-term relationships while still in school. Now he was on the other side of the country from his family and not finding the partner he wanted.

At work, Martin got a nudge from Jim, his boss, to talk to me. Jim and I were friends. Jim's wife set me up on a couple of blind dates that went nowhere. When Martin suggested we go to lunch, I assumed it was to talk about a competing company which several of our co-workers started. I knew they were raiding the ranks. He stopped me in the hall at work.

"I think we should go to lunch," he said.

"Okay," I said.

"Tomorrow?" he asked.

"Sure, noon," I said.

At lunch, I ordered a salad, and he ordered a sandwich. He asked about my interests outside of work, and we hit all the highlights of small talk. I was surprised as lunch ended, and we headed back to work; no question about the other company had come up.

That lunch was the first of many and eventually, I told him about my assumption.

He shrugged and said no one from that company had approached him. "In a meeting, I listened and was amazed to hear someone speak so logically. I looked and saw that it was you. I wanted to get to know you."

That is what he told me. It was what I wanted to hear. I had been on dates where the guy got excited

10

when he saw my car – I was driving a 240Z then. I wanted to be sought for who I was, not what I drove.

We spent time getting to know one another over lunch that spring and summer. Whenever I visited the Engineering building, he would jump up from his seat and meet me in the hallway. Did he listen for my voice? I put his name on an invitation to my boss's pool party. He was amazed that he was one of the few engineers invited to the Sales Department party. When he realized that I was the one who invited him, things heated up.

"I think we should go away for a weekend together," he suggested one day.

"Where?" I asked.

"Is the destination critical?"

"Not really," I said.

"Leave it to me. I'll arrange the whole thing."

"What should I pack?" I asked hoping for a hint to the destination.

"I'll make you a list," he said. The list followed and included a bathing suit, formal gown, shorts, sneakers, sunglasses, floppy hat.

On Friday, we left work together and drove to the airport.

"Where are we going?" I asked.

"You'll see," he said.

I told myself it didn't matter, we would have fun. Martin parked in the lot, and we rode the shuttle back to the terminal. He seemed troubled. He looked out the window and fidgeted.

I took his hand, "Is something the matter."

"Well," he said, "I've been busy and never actually made any arrangements."

"Where were we going?" I asked.

I was surprised that he had put forth all this mystery but never followed through.

He shrugged. "I don't know. You got any ideas?"

"I think we should buy tickets for the next flight out to a destination starting with the letter … L," I said, surprising myself. Why L? What were the options? Los Angeles, Las Vegas, Louisiana? I would like to go there, never been.

"Okay," he said.

At the ticket counter, the first flight to a destination starting with L was Los Angeles, and we bought tickets and were in the air within the hour.

Landing, we selected a hotel with airport pickup. The evening gown never left the suitcase, but we swam, visited amusement parks, rode the roller coasters (which we both loved) and talked and talked and fell further in love.

In our first year together, we flew to Hawaii, a first for each of us. Little did we realize that on that trip, we conceived our son. When I was pregnant, Martin spoiled me rotten, offered to run out and satisfy whatever craving I had. He made me feel special every day. We loved and cared for each other. Our family unit changed with the birth of Sam. To that point, we divided all the expenses, his vs. mine. But when his son was born, we split all the costs down the middle including my mortgage. For him, having a son cemented us together as a family. We started talking about marriage, and he bought me an engagement ring.

Martin felt estranged from his father, but his father couldn't wait to come and stay with us, sleeping on the hide-a-bed to be near his first grandchild. This was a two-fold blessing for Martin, to father the first grandchild and to be seen in this light by his father. The estrangement and resentment Martin felt, dissipated. His father and stepmother became closer to us, attending our wedding and regularly visiting to spend time with the grandchildren, accepting my son as another grandchild. We were a happy family.

Even with two small children, we traveled, taking them to movies, to Disneyland and the World's Fair in Vancouver. As the children grew, we outgrew our little house and moved into another, and a few years later, we doubled our family with the birth of twin sons.

I remember calling Martin at work as I left the doctor's office. "We need to buy a new car," I said.

"Why?" he asked.

"Your car only seats four, and mine five," I said.

"So?"

"We need a bigger car. We're having twins; there will be six of us now."

There was a lot of talk about the twins before they arrived. "Is there a history of twins in the family?" "Will they be identical?" "Why twins?" Martin and I counted back the days and laughed when we realized that we had probably conceived them on a night in April. I had come to bed tired and hot. The windows were open, but still, the ninety-degree air clung to my skin. He turned to me, amorous intentions on his mind.

"It's too hot for sex," I said.

"C'mon," he said.

"Let's go outside. It's cooler in the backyard."

"Really?"

I didn't think he'd do it. But he rose, and we dragged the comforter off the bed and out into the backyard beneath the willow tree. We lay down in the cool of the night.

Later, when a gardener explained that we should remove the willow tree to make room for a replanting, we looked at each other and in unison said, "No, that tree stays."

We worked together for several years at the company where we met, and during that time we were the darlings. My ten years of seniority in a fledgling startup kept me in the know, and Martin was the brilliant mind behind the new computer product. After changes in the market and key personnel, we moved on to new jobs. We sorted out what needed to be done together and enjoyed our family life.

From the very beginning our relationship was grounded in intellect. Martin appreciated my intelligence and sense of logic; I was amazed by the breadth and depth of his knowledge. We enjoyed conversing on everything, books, movies, politics, economics. We sat in front of the television watching *Jeopardy* and shouted out the answers, often responding before the contestants. We were raised in different faiths but agreed on basic tenets without feeling a need or desire to participate in socialized religions. We wanted to expose our children to as much knowledge and information as we could, allowing them to make their own choices.

We didn't argue or fight. Occasionally there were misunderstandings, after which one of us pouted or stomped about, but after a breather, we would discuss and resolve. What relationship doesn't have those challenges that require one or both to change and back down or accept the wants of the other? I did not stop and wonder if I had made a mistake. I tended to count all the things about us that were right.

I was drawn to Martin because of his self-assurance and confidence. I didn't feel that I had that, I questioned myself, where did I fit, was I smart enough. Some people told me he was arrogant; we would laugh at that, considering that the speaker was jealous or frightened by his knowledge and confidence. Martin often sought my advice on how to deal with matters; how he should deal with a difficult boss, issues with employees. Not only did he ask, but he also took my advice, and thanked me when it resulted positively.

With both of us working high stress managerial jobs, and four small children, our lives were full and busy. Kids up, dressed, fed, and dropped at day care and/or school, then on to work. At the end of the day, the reverse commute, fighting traffic, picking up the kids, dinner, dishes, homework, laundry. There was less and less time for us.

I remember whining over the division of labor. Martin generated a spreadsheet of all the various household tasks, and weighted them by complexity, duration, and boringness. Even when he added what he was doing and what additional duties he would take on, the division was nowhere near equal.

"It's what I can do," he said, "and no more."

I stood holding the list. Martin spent hours on this, and I could have used his help instead with laundry. I stepped back and sucked it up; this is what my mother would have done, I justified it to myself. "Not everything is fair," was my father's lesson for me.

Martin explained, "It's better for me to hold myself in reserve for when you get so overworked you can't continue, then I can step in."

"But why not help me now so that I won't get there."

He shrugged, and we were at an impasse.

16

I wanted everything neat and clean and tried to keep up. When I asked him to help, he hired a cleaning service.

But as anyone knows who hires a cleaning service, if you don't put things where you want them, they may be lost. So, I got all the complaints about the things they moved, but he would make no effort to pick up after himself.

The boys were responsible for their rooms, and I would work with them to keep them in order. Eventually, they learned to do their own laundry. Better to raise boys to men who could look after themselves and not feel that they needed someone to do their laundry and cooking.

All this led to less time for the two of us. After work, I'd change out of my business attire and suggest he keep me company in the kitchen, but he preferred to relax on the bed in front of the television. Martin suffered from an old back injury, and it was better to lie down than sit, besides he had been sitting all day at work. Another impasse. I would push it aside. What couple didn't have these problems with kids and work and not enough time?

From this distant side of the looking glass, I see now the signs that pointed toward disaster. At the time I thought what relationship doesn't have its ups and downs, and bumps in the road? We worked out what we could, and in truth, ignored the rest, if it could be circumvented. I asked myself, what constitutes wrong? What is normal, what is not? Nothing that Martin said or did during all those years prepared me for what was to come.

The oddities that did occur pointed to some internal issues that plagued him.

The first time I witnessed this, we jointly hosted a costume party before he moved in with me. Everyone was to come dressed as their fantasy. Why we selected that I don't recall, and how we dressed seemed to have little to do with our own fantasies. I remember our friend Herb, an accountant, coming with his girlfriend. They both came dressed as women, and at some point that evening, she sat down and painted nail polish on Herb's nails. Martin seemed surprised and overly curious. He sat watching them mesmerized.

"I can't believe he's letting her do that," he said. But he sat and watched her paint his fingernails and toenails.

I expected a romantic ending to the evening but instead played nurse to his anguish. He suffered what I would come to know as a panic attack when his boss noted his piano and asked if he played. Learning that he did, he repeatedly tried to coerce him to play. Martin's fear of making an error stupefied him. I remember being the caretaker but not understanding what was so bothersome. He played for me and after years of classical training, played very well. But his fear of making a mistake kept him from performing in front of others.

The second time he seemed immobilized by fear was perhaps a year later when Martin invited another boss and engineering team to our home for dinner. I cooked and was serving it when he disappeared. Everyone was seated at the table, and I searched for him. I found him in bed.

"What are you doing?" I asked.

"I don't feel well."

"But everyone is at the table now … to eat."

"I can't," he said.

"But they are your guests. Just sit with us." I tried to find a middle ground.

"No." He turned away from me.

I took my seat, made an apology, and carried on. The hardest part was that he was on the other side of the dining room wall, less than six feet away from where I sat entertaining his guests.

Later, I tried to understand what happened. Martin reluctantly told me that when his boss saw the grand piano, he asked him to play after dinner, and he bolted.

While these instances were nothing more than that, they pointed toward something I should have paid more attention to. I didn't.

Martin told me he started college as a premed student and wanted to be a doctor, but a low grade in one class panicked him, so he dropped the class and changed his major.

"We marry the men who are most unlike our father, and we divorce them because they are not like our father," I told my sister to help console her after her divorce. She reminded me of it years later, and I sat digesting it slowly.

"Yes, that is true," I said.

"I know," she said, "He was so much fun and talkative, but he wouldn't do the simplest things, like pay bills, return borrowed items … do what he was supposed to do."

"You know we really should spend more time studying the parents of the men we fall in love with."

"You're right."

What did my parents imprint on me? My father must have said five million times "life is not fair." I got tired of hearing it, but he was trying to teach me that just because something is unfair, does not mean it will not happen. My father ruled sternly and stoically, doling out equality about the age of permission to ride a bicycle, take driver instruction, and assistance when we purchased our first cars.

My mother's lessons came as I followed in her footsteps. If something needs to be done, you do it; you don't complain. Both my parents were stoic. You suck it up; you take it, you move forward no matter.

You just do it. You don't throw in the towel; you don't turn and run.

When my father served in the Navy during World War II, two ships he served on were sunk. He was responsible for the ship's log and in both instances, he got off the ship with the log in hand. He never spoke of his experiences other than that one story which was relayed to us.

The question was how would these characteristics play out in our lives? Would they affect our relationship? For better or worse?

I watched as three of my sisters suffered through divorce and stood firm in their support. Martin and I talked about how strong our relationship was and how we would share our lives together.

"We are family," he said over and over.

There are photos of the boys romping in the backyard. They were so young, playing with the hose, riding tricycles. As the pages flip, they are on skates and bicycles. Then one by one they go through soccer and birthday parties.

The years fly by.

Each Thanksgiving we posed on the stairway of our home and the photograph captured the six faces of our family. The best of these photos would become our Christmas card for that year. The album of the first ten years of our life together is complete. I took a long look at the last picture of our smiling faces.

Everything was not perfect, but we learned to negotiate the parts that were not. We worked well together and raising our four sons was our common goal.

It is always so easy to look back and see signs that should have pointed you in a different direction. Those panic atacks that he had, his inability to cope with the fear of making a mistake pointed to something. So afraid to make an error didn't seem to halt his transition though.

While he offered to come up with a great getaway for us but never did – He would whine about needing a vacation and then let me plan one without any feedback but upon the return he would give me an earful of what was wrong with it.

Too late I learned that I was dealing with a narcissist who wanted to take the easiest path and would circumvent criticism. I ask myself what lesson I was supposed to learn to get through this.

Into the Rabbit Hole

We had been living together for ten years. It was two thirty in the morning, and we were sitting on the floor in our walk-in closet. Just completed was the assembly of the power wheels car for our five-year-old twin sons' birthday surprise. All we had to do was push it out of the bedroom and into the living room. Then we could go to bed.

"There is something I want to tell you," he started.

"Yes…" I said.

"This is hard for me," he said.

"What?" I said. I wanted to climb into bed and go to sleep. The kids would be up in less than three hours. It was Christmas, and we had a twelve-year-old, an eight-year-old and the five-year-olds.

"Well, I would like to have your help."

"What?" My impatience was growing. I do not do well late at night.

"I want to dress up in women's clothes," he blurted out.

As I sat there surrounded by my clothing; dresses and skirts, business suits and blouses, leggings and sweaters, boots and heels; I recoiled.

Swoop right down the rabbit hole. One minute I was sitting in my closet with my husband and the next minute I was with someone I did not recognize. I was afraid and on unknown terrain. I don't remember how that got resolved. It just got said, then we both shut it up, and tiptoed around it like a present that would never be unwrapped.

Years passed.

I told people that I was in the rapid response business because I fulfilled whims in a short period of time. Specifically, I created and delivered gift baskets for corporate clients.

After being laid off from my high-tech marketing position, I took some time. One day Martin suggested that maybe I should go into business for myself rather than working for someone. He didn't say much else but left me on my own. I did some research about businesses you could start and looked inside myself to see what I could get excited about. For twenty years I had worked for computer manufacturers who sold their products to OEM suppliers, so I longed for something more consumer oriented and something that would fulfill my creative nature. Once I stumbled on the idea of gift baskets, I was hooked. Soon after I found a listing for one that was up for sale. Further study led me to conclude the purchase of the business which was located in the heart of Silicon Valley had a strong customer base in those companies. Unlike most of the competition at the time, I had enough business to work the Monday through Friday week without weekends and to have a staff of three or four people.

Everything we did was custom, and I loved the one on one of working directly with my clients. After a particularly rapid response when I had to whip up a tub filled with fifty bottles of beer on ice and deliver it, I pulled over to the side of the road.

Cell phones were the up and coming "have to haves" and mine was ringing. It was a call from my husband, Martin.

" I got the results," he said

"Yes…" I said.

It's cancer. Lymphoma," he said. "They sent me to an oncologist. I have an appointment next week. I was so stunned, I called Dr. Norris, and he said to come right in. I just left his office. He was very kind. I'm glad we picked him as our family doctor."

"Are you on your way home? I'll be home in about an hour." I told him.

"I think we got it early enough." He said.

"I am sure. Love you. See you soon." I said.

I sat there on the side of the road, forehead into the steering wheel hub and sobbed. It was October fifth, two years to the day after my father died from cancer. That cancer had come on and spent twelve years playing hide and seek. I had been there to support my mother as my father died.

In such instances, I always said there was a reason. That I would now have to be there for my husband to go through the same thing was not a good enough reason.

A lot of positive things happened because he had cancer: his father and stepmother became more involved in our lives, family members pulled together. Everyone emailed with alternative medicines and approaches to fighting lymphoma. His peers were very supportive, and his employer was generous. His hair went and came again. Then one doctor said that the chemo didn't work, and that he didn't know what else to do. But another doctor examined him and declared that he was cured. Just as arbitrary as one pill makes you large and one makes you small.

The white rabbit ran through clutching his watch and crying "I'm late, I'm late for a very important date."

"Ever since I had to face my own death, I knew that I could not ignore what I wanted or put it off any longer," Martin told me one night.

"What?" I said. I was clueless.

"I want to be a woman," he said, "I've been reading about it on the internet."

I stared at him in disbelief. Over and over again I had asked him if that was why he wanted to dress in woman's clothing. Again and again, he said no, it was just for fun.

He tried to soften the blow. "Unless I can be a good-looking woman, I will not go through with it, but I have to try."

Those words were saved for replay, and I would repeat them to myself during the coming years.

Saying I was unprepared sounds like an understatement, now. I felt like Alice falling down the rabbit hole into an entirely different life. Even if I could find my way out, could my life continue as it had been? I cried, feeling my perfect life slipping away.

When an event occurs that knocks you down, you will eventually look into the rear-view mirror and wonder how you missed the clues. He used to tell me the story about how his father had wanted a son and told his mother when she was pregnant with him.

"It had better be a boy."

What a silly thing, I thought.

And then he would say to me, "You don't have to worry because I am all man."

"Of course, you are, what else would you be?" I said.

There was the naïve Alice looking back at me. One pill makes you large, and one pill makes you small. Today one pill makes you male, another makes you female. Here sits the Mad Hatter dispensing the pills from unmarked bottles without childproof caps.

I felt blindsided by his confession. I could not make sense of it. He was not feminine. My understanding of anything not "normal" was vague and lost in the shadows.

I learned that while I have no problem initiating change, I rebel at any change thrust upon me.

Alone

Traumatized children pour out their pain in drawings that help professionals understand them. In my picture, I am in the center holding on, and being pulled apart. Atlas with the weight of the world on my shoulders. A cat hanging by its claws.

During the next few years I was in shock. I remember things, activities, and words but I no longer comprehend that we lived our lives as if there was nothing going horribly wrong. I was sworn to secrecy and silence. I told no one.

My goal was to protect the children and allow them to continue in their idealized world and hope that we would get them into adulthood before anything had to be revealed. I silently prayed to God to make this all go away, make it be a residual

29

reaction to all the chemotherapy. If nothing else let Martin come to see that he would not be the beautiful woman that he so longed to be.

To be fair, I was buried in busyness. I ran the household, had my gift basket business with five employees, and I was a road warrior for selling services to venture capital-backed startups managing sales offices across the US. There wasn't time to deal with it. Traveling gave me relief.

Martin handled the bills, so I didn't see the money being spent on electrolysis and laser hair removal. When I would climb into bed next to him after a week away, I would be shocked to find a new hairless area. Blindfolded I could no longer pick out my husband in a lineup of naked men.

My husband started down the approved path that took him through the maze that led to the surgeon's table. Like painting white roses red, it takes more than makeup to make a man into a woman. That first year you work with a counselor who helps sort out your feelings. There are group sessions where guest speakers come in to instruct how to present as a woman.

Imagine a 1950s charm school course for teenage girls that is being administered to forty to sixty-year-old men. They learn how to dress, walk, talk, how to do their hair, makeup, and personal hygiene.

Then they will need to get consent from a second counselor that they are indeed a candidate for gender re-assignment.

The secrecy was getting to me. In honoring my husband, I had taken this vow of silence, but I am a collaborative person who shares ideas and thoughts. I was pouring out my heart in documents that never left the computer.

Humor is my sanity keeper. When he began to take hormones and talk incessantly about his emergence as a woman and wearing women's clothing, I would tell myself the same joke over and over again.

"I am waiting for the other shoe to drop, and I am hoping it will not be a pump." I typed that when I heard someone smirk.

Panic struck. If it were my husband reading over my shoulder, he would be hurt by my self-pitying words, but I couldn't believe that he was up this early in the morning. If it were one of the kids, then they would be full of questions about the fiction I was writing. I sucked in my breath like a warrior raises his shield, and slowly swiveled to meet who was behind me. There was no one. I did a complete three-sixty, and there was no one.

"Whew," I released the breath.

Again, there came the smirk. I swung the chair around and again caught no one reading over my shoulder.

"Well?" I sighed.

"Well, what?" came an echo.

"Who?"

"Who Who?" Again, an echo.

Goosebumps rose all over my body. This was indeed weird. Someone was answering me back, but there was no one in view. I sat back down and closed the window.

"Oh, Boo Hoo," came the voice

"Show yourself," I demanded.

I was sitting looking at my desktop and there in the upper right-hand corner was a big grin staring back at me. I wondered if this was some new Microsoft icon helper like the bendy paperclip.

"Well," I said. "So, there you are."

"Well, yourself."

"Why are you here?

"You were making me laugh."

"Good enough. Can you make me laugh?"

"Keep it up; you are doing a pretty good job yourself."

"Do you have the answers?"

"Do you really want the answers?"

"Yes."

"Then keep looking."

"What help is that?"

"It is what you asked for?"

As I stared in amazement, it faded away with a soft chuckle.

Of course, this was all in my head – but it provided me with an imaginary friend to ponder that stray question that wandered through my subconscious. Having to keep the secret and not being able to talk with my support group, friends and family, isolated me.

Enter the Queen

What you don't know is always worse than what you do know. The unknown is the scariest course we set. My husband began to prattle on about transgenders, transsexuals, transvestites and cross dressers. Try as I felt that I should, I could not comprehend, and tugging at the back of my mind was the question of whether or not he was out of his mind. That would be the easy way out.

I sought out third parties to try and get a handle on what he was talking about. If he was working with two therapists, there ought to be another one I could go to. If he was finding information on the Internet, then I should also. So, in the quiet of early morning when I was the only one up and about, I sat down at the keyboard and began my research.

I easily found a list of counselors, a blessing to living in the third largest city in California. I needed to understand the clinical viewpoint on what was going on and where the boundaries might indicate that he was indeed crazy. I had been to psychiatrists before about his depression — I knew I could not fix it but had learned how to establish boundaries so that I didn't wear myself out.

I would meet with Kathryn Steiner, a gender dysphasia counselor on the Stanford Medical Center campus three times. I asked my questions.

"How long does this pouty teenager phase last?"

"Usually, it will subside within two years following surgery," she said.

"How do I deal with the fact that I have lost my husband and there is this new person there?"

"I can't say. That is up to each couple. The man you married is still in there, but right now he is a teenage girl."

"How many women stay?" I wondered, but too afraid to ask this question.

"Again, it depends on the couple – but not many." She confided.

I had cried all I could cry in front of a stranger. I felt that I had asked all the questions I could conjure up. There was no map for a way out of this maze; I would have to go slowly, trial and error, and with patience. She got up and crossed the room to bring me a box of tissues. I had been wondering how a woman feels about watching these men sort out their dreams to become women. How would I feel if I were not so personally involved? In the last session, we had talked about some of the transgendered she counseled and had laughed at their inappropriate dress. I thought of the dresses that my husband was buying on eBay and hanging on my side of the closet. Ugly stepsister dresses was how I thought of them. Gaudy, scanty and inappropriate were fitting adjectives for each of them.

I watched Kathryn bend over and pick up the box. I envied her being thin, having almost no hips. I noted then that her dress was just a bit too provocative for a counselor. It was more cocktail than professional, spaghetti straps and short skirt. Hadn't we just talked about inappropriate dress?

As she handed me the box, I sniffled and blew my nose, and looked down at her shoes. They were lime green satin slip-on mules with rhinestones. Something that you would wear to a cocktail party; not sit in counseling sessions.

I looked into her face again: less feminine, heavy on the eye liner, bleached blonde hair; a little too long for a middle-aged psychologist. Suddenly I felt duped again. I imagined that the Queen of Hearts appeared behind her and yelled "Off with her shoes!" The psychologist was a trans person as well. I scampered out of the rabbit hole.

I never learned if my assumptions about the counselor were accurate but this demonstrates my need to feel secure and safe when looking for help. I truly felt lost in a world where everyone could be other than what I thought. As if the whole world was not what I had come to rely on. As a friend said, the adult version of the child learning there is no Santa Claus.

The Mad Hatter's Tea Party

I stumbled across an online support group for trans families which included the entire gambit: gays and lesbians as well as the trans and their family members. I had no idea who these people were and what help they might offer. I had to fill out a form and submit "my story" before anyone would contact me. I took a deep breath, hoped for salvation, and hit the enter key.

That afternoon I received an email welcoming me to the group and notification that I had been added to the email and could now post. To my surprise, I also received an email introducing me by way of "my story."

Within minutes I began to receive emails from other women who were in similar situations. I had joined the Mad Hater's Tea Party and what a wonderful place it was. We were from all over the globe, and all ages but most were like me. We had two things in common: first, we were women, and our husbands wanted to be women, and second, that they came out to us about ten years into the relationship. Most women were in their fifties or sixties. We were the ones who had not spat in their face and thrown them out when they told us but had tried to keep it together.

These women would become my fuel. We read each other's questions and poured out our hopes and fears supporting one another. We clinked our teacups to one another and moved down to make room for new members every day. We often had members who had reached their breaking points and left. They didn't just leave the support group; they left their marriage, their lives as they had known them, and struck out to find themselves again. With each "goodbye" I wondered about whether it was better to stay or better to go.

I felt that I was ostracized from my own life. I was no longer a woman married to a man. I was about to be a woman married to a woman. Did this make me lesbian? Labels are not the thing that I was concerned about; it is that once down the rabbit hole I was unable to find my bearings.

But I was not alone in losing my bearings. One other woman in our trans family group wrote about her circumstances. She and her partner are lesbians she wrote, however, her partner had begun to transition to male. As lesbians, they were already minority status but now as her Vicky was becoming Richard, they were cast out of the lesbian society for being in a heterosexual relationship. Now she didn't know where she belonged. I totally understood her confusion and felt for her loss. I abhor exclusionary action. What could be worse than to be cast out from an alternative lifestyle for not being alternative enough? I could feel the rumble underfoot and knew the Queen of Hearts was on a rampage.

I began to see how I was not alone in this circumstance. There were many more women like me with husbands who wanted to be women. How we dealt with it was different and as individual as we are. Over time I learned that I had the power to place limits and boundaries. Up until I did, I was lost.

Mirror Image

Some mirrors are like those distorted ones at carnivals.

I imagine Martin looked into the mirror and only saw what he wanted to see. He viewed his dark brown eyes with the long lashes and creamy skin. He avoided the beard stubble, the heavy brow, the square jaw, and prominent chin. He probably imagined turtlenecks to hide his Adam's apple and low-cut bodices to show off the breasts he would someday have. He didn't see the hairy chest or the rapidly retreating hairline and the thinning out of what hair he had. He looked at the soft dark curls that reached down his neck and touched his shirt collar and, imagined that soon they would cover his whole scalp.

He would look at a photo of his mother when she was about twenty and think that he would look like her. At least that is what he wanted.

He went through his daily routine: pee, pull on underwear, a short sleeve cotton shirt, the same polyester pants he wore daily to work. He ran a comb through his hair quickly, so he wouldn't have to address reality. He'd cross to the bed, sitting on the edge and pull on his black cotton socks, then cram his feet into his New Balance athletic shoes without having to untie or retie them. He'd get into his car and drive to work. That was his routine; it took ten minutes from bed to the door. That was his whole getting ready for work routine.

I knew this routine like I knew my own. I grimaced at the steps he missed and wondered how he could ever make the leap to being a woman. I talked to him about the care he should give his appearance. I recommended that he brush his teeth.

"Why?" He asked. "I haven't eaten anything since I brushed them last night."

I pointed out to him that he wore the same pair of pants Monday through Friday each week. He should change every day.

"Why?" He asked "I haven't spilled anything on them, and I wear underwear. That seems illogical."

I was caught in the illogic of his two worlds. In one he was a techno-geek nerd with all the stereotypical trappings including the clothing and hygiene. In the other, he lusted to be a beautiful woman. I couldn't connect the dots. His words echoed in my head.

"If I cannot be a good-looking woman then I will not do it."

Is that the way out of all of this? Let him try, and when he sees that he cannot achieve what he wants, he will relent.

* * *

I caught him standing behind me watching me as I put on my makeup. Once, I thought this was how he appreciated me. Now I realized that he stored this away as an instruction. I wondered how many of these he remembered.

Playboy magazines were stacked on the floor on his side of the bed along with the PCWorld and Integrated Circuit data sheets. I thought I understood how men had to have those photos of young, naked women to amuse themselves. I suddenly flashed back to those photos and began to wonder if when he looked at them and lay there touching himself if he was thinking of how he would feel when he had a body like the one he was looking at. I had been offended because I thought he lusted after them and not me. Now I realized he lusted after the woman inside himself.

Beyond the rabbit hole, I was now slipping down a slope into a place I didn't want to go. I must shake it off, change the channel and move back into my world of busyness. It was safe there. I knew who I was and what I should do.

As a child I tried to make sense of everything. Our parents teach us about much, but sometimes we make up our own rules about how things work. As an adult we reflect back on these myths we carry and realize that we did not understand and correct. I don't know when or why Martin felt that he should be a girl, but he never seemed to vacillate on that once he began to speak of it. Makes me wonder how many people feel that they should be other than they are.

And makes me happy and content in being me the way I am now.

The Big Box of Crayons

As the police advanced on the protesters and used their brute strength, the television cameras captured it all, and the fury between my father and I seemed to reach its apex. For some time, I railed against my father and his inflexibleness which to me was in terms of black or white. This had nothing to do with race. To him everything was either right or wrong; there was no gray area. It was the end of the 60s and freedom was spewing forth; there was a lot of room for every color and every viewpoint. I remember watching the Democratic convention until it was only coverage of the unrest in the streets, I yelled something at my father and with tears streaming, stormed out of the house. I was nineteen, starting to form my own opinions but not having the maturity to realize that I was still speaking in an adolescence tongue. My father tried to point the right way to me, but I was beyond reason.

I thought of this as I began to learn about transsexuals, transgenders, transvestites and crossdressers. My father's inflexibleness came back to me whenever I sought normalcy. To me, men were supposed to be men and attracted to women; women were women and attracted to men.

What I found was as many variations to this as there are colors in a big box of crayons. It is, in fact, a continuum, without end. Men are attracted to men, to women, to both, to neither, and without sexual orientation at all. Women are attracted to women, to men, to both, to neither and without sexual orientation. There are male bodies with male traits, male bodies with female traits and the same for women. If you think up a permutation, it exists. So, what is normal? Is there a right and a wrong? Is it all black or white or is it okay that every color is fully represented in this life?

I would learn that transsexuals may be of either gender who dress as their opposite and are sexually aroused in the dressing, while crossdressers are similar but without the sexual arousal. Transgenders are those where the sexual orientation and the body are not in sync, and these are the ones who seek sexual reassignment surgery to align their orientation with their body. Males that are males that are attracted to other males are called homosexuals. A transgendered woman may feel that she should be male, will undergo surgery and take hormones and will become male and may still be attracted to men, therefore, changing her from a heterosexual to a homosexual.

My husband believed that he was a woman trapped in a man's body. He wanted to have his male genitalia removed and create the physical body of a woman. He felt that he was still attracted to women and not to men; however, he had a growing desire to know what it felt like to be on the receiving end of male passion.

"I love you and want to spend the rest of my life with you," he told me. "But I am curious and would at least once like to have a man make love to me."

Swoop down the rabbit hole. The quotation balloon hung suspended in the air.

The Cheshire cat grinned at me. "What did you think was going to happen? Did you think that he would go to she and everything else would stay the same?"

I did not believe that I had thought that, but he had said it would be so. How much did he tell me that had not come to pass? Did he intentionally lie, or did he tell me things so that I would stay?

"That's more like it," said the cat reading my thoughts. The grin hung in the air, but the body of the cat disappeared.

There are a lot of things we never want to tell our parents. My father died before Martin revealed his wanting to dress in women's clothing. I was in silence mode when my mother died just five months later. They would have been shocked but supportive of me. I am thankful for my sisters who always offer a shoulder and a hand.

I cannot emphasize enough how important it is to not walk this path alone. Whether you are the one caught in the web or simply an onlooker, seek a support team.

Standards of Care

There are standards of care for transgendered people who want to transition. These were created to set guidelines and to control access to health services. The trend was moving toward informed consent for adults, where health services would be provided once the client acknowledged they were aware of the potential benefits and drawbacks. As more people opt for these consent programs standards of care would decline in importance, thus allowing clients to move at their own speed. For Martin, there were rules he had to follow.

The original standards of care were a set of guidelines devised and maintained by the Harry Benjamin International Gender Dysphoria Association. They were drafted in 1979 as protocol for dealing with gender identity therapy and care, although they came under fire in recent years for not representing the wishes of those they were designed to serve. In 2006 they changed their name to World Professional Association for Transgender Health.

When Martin entered this process, he had tot be interviewed by a psychologist who would explore and confirm (or deny) the existence of gender confusion or dysphoria, then he could begin working with a gender therapist. For him, it was easy to find one locally and to become enrolled in her group of twenty transsexuals. Together they would learn how to deal with their feelings and learn how to dress, act, and speak as a woman. Being able to pass as female is critical to the success of such a transition. While under the guidance of the gender therapist, Martin was prescribed the hormone estrogen, and this countered testosterone and induced breast growth. With the removal of the testes and therefore, no longer testosterone production, his body would take on more feminine physical characteristics.

The next hurdle would be to have the approval of two separate gender counselors that he was fit for gender reassignment.

But there was one more hurdle after that: you had to live as a woman 24/7 for one year.

Even as I read about the standards of care, I could see that Martin was looking to improve the timeline, speed up the process. Still, I could count on two or three more years before I would have to deal with the reality of him becoming a woman. If I could forestall it another two years, our children would be grown, out of high school. I worried about how this would affect them in their early teens.

From the first time Martin explained this to me, I had misgivings about his willingness to follow the rules. He was someone who took short cuts, the easier way, and self-prescribed medication.

It seemed like he was looking for an answer but I supported him and hoped that he was working on a real answer for himself.

When I saw that he didn't follow through or bypassed a step, I felt like the disciplinarian pointing out the rules over and over again. This was not the role I wanted. Nor did he.

Why Now?

I was truly surprised to learn that the group Martin would be meeting with twice a month was comprised of twenty males identifying as female and all were in their late 40s or early 50s. They represented a wide range of careers, the majority of them engineers like Martin. Some were hands-on workers, like mechanics, but there were also a few who had never quite found a place and held minimum wage jobs.

My research further surprised me. When I asked, "Why now?" One gender therapist reported that in her experience, there were several universal impetuses. The first was that the person had always been aware of this gender confusion and was motivated to do something now because of a change in a relationship. They had just ended a relationship or had lost a close family member which then begged the question, "Why not now?"

Debilitating depression marked the turning point for others.

While Martin would tell me that as a young boy, he watched the Mickey Mouse Club and wanted to wear the cowgirl outfit, not the one the boys wore, he did not exhibit any feminine characteristics. He was not obsessed with clothing or how he looked. Perhaps it was internalized and his approach to dressing was bland because he was limited to the male wardrobe. This impulse had been present in his life for a long time, the fact that he had not acted on it during the first ten years of our relationship was how hidden he kept it. He did not act on it, nor did he ever discuss it with me prior to that night in the closet.

Raised in the Midwest and working on the East Coast after college, it became his desire to move to the San Francisco Bay Area. That choice had to be because of the freer lifestyle and acceptance.

The impetus for Martin was his brush with cancer. While it had not been near death, he did share with me that if he died, he would regret never acting on his desire to be a woman. I was affected by his depression and wondered if the cause was based in his gender confusion.

Twist & Shout

If I were to chart the twists and turns that got me to this point in the maze, would I be able to find my way back? That was the question. I sat on the floor of my closet under the skirts of my dresses. I pulled a comforter off the linen shelf and wrapped it around myself. I did not want to be in the bedroom with him, but there was nowhere else to go.

As I reflected, I saw that he persuasively manipulated me to where I sat cowering. He knew my weaknesses and played me along. Perhaps he did not do this purposefully, but his emotions were being ruled by the hormones.

Once he started taking the estrogen, he began to develop breasts and took on the attitude of a teenage girl.

One night he shook my shoulder, waking me.

"What?" I said.

"I can't sleep," he said.

"What's wrong?" I asked. He rarely did this. Was the cancer back?

"I think I did something I shouldn't," he said.

"What?" I wondered what was important enough to wake me.

"I ordered drugs online."

"What are you worried about?" I didn't think he was ordering heroin or other illegal substances. What was he talking about? Was there a darker side I didn't know about?

"I bought hormones … estrogen," he said.

I flashed back to when my OB/GYN had prescribed estrogen for me after the hysterectomy. At that time Martin was on Prozac for depression. I would count out his pills when his mood changed, assessing whether or not he was taking his medication. I did not refill my prescription for estrogen because I feared that he would take them, or worse, had replaced my pills with something else.

"I keep fearing that someone will come to the house and arrest you." He continued.

"Me? Why would they arrest me?"

"Because I ordered them in your name," he said.

"Stop using my name," I said. "Perhaps you need to set up the appointment with the counselor and start on the path to being able to have hormones prescribed."

I rose from the bed and walked through the house, letting this conversation sink in. I received copies of catalogs for post mastectomy prosthetics and big and tall women's lingerie. I tossed them believing them to be spam mail, but I saw my name on the address labels. Martin was usually home first and got the mail. What else was he doing in my name?

As this information began to sink in, I was horrified, then rightly indignant. He was using my name to get what he wanted. Was he...had he been using me all along to get to this point? Was I not the beloved but the duped? Now when I watch movies about a gay man who marries to hide his homosexuality, I twitch as this thought replays itself in my head.

Did I ever truly know what I meant to him?

Straddling Two Realities

Somedays felt as if nothing was wrong while others left me cowering under the blankets. What I remember are those things that seemed so out of place. These specific instances reflected the growing uneasiness about the uncertain future.

On one occasion, we traveled with the kids to my sister's wedding. I wore a dress, and he complained about my lack of style. He usually noted that my clothes were too colorful. He wore his signature outfit, only now he wore a black sports bra under his shirt to bind his burgeoning breasts. That is what a little estrogen will do to a man.

The kids were excited to have a pool at the hotel, but Dad could not go in the pool because of those breasts. That was the first time, he didn't swim with the kids. I was afraid that all their questions would be the undoing, but a curt "no" from him was all it took.

* * *

Imagine my fence walking when I must remind my husband to wear dark colored shirts so that his sports bra will not show through. I continually nagged him to keep his socks on at all times because while he had a coat of clear polish on his ever-lengthening fingernails, his toes were painted red. When the relatives gathered to enjoy breakfast, he ordered his food to the room and redid his pedicure. He secreted himself away in our room and had no less nor no more social interaction than usual.

It wasn't that he was antisocial as much as that if he wasn't the center of attention, he wasn't interested in making small talk. Of course, at the time, this wasn't all that clear to me.

* * *

I moved between the world where I didn't acknowledge what was going on and keeping the secret, and the world where my husband was becoming a woman. With me, he talked about clothes and makeup and told me we were like best girlfriends. I didn't know how to correct that statement because BFFs go both ways not just one.

58

* * *

I remember another wedding. The son of a friend invited us to an informal outdoor wedding. We sat on wooden folding chairs in the heat of the day. I was embarrassed and protective at the same time. I knew that he had breasts that he tried to hide under a sport bra and a baggy shirt. He wore his black cotton socks and athletic shoes, but I knew that his toenails were painted blood red He wore men's polyester pants but probably wore women's panties as well. And it became easier for me to sit by him and be quiet than to be myself.

"When I am a woman, I will wear boots," he leaned over and whispered to me.

"Boots?"

"Yes. They will look hot and will hide my big calves."

"Even in summer?"

"Sure, boots are great. Why not?"

I wiped the sweat from my brow. Our average summer temp was in the 90s and I couldn't contemplate boots with a sundress.

* * *

Then his parents suggested a winter holiday in Florida. Again, we had an awkward moment when everyone put on their bathing suits and headed to the beach, but Martin hung back and made some lame excuse. What were we thinking to plan this week-long trip where he cannot take off his shirt and swim? I don't think anyone remembered or commented on that. What everyone remembered was the contents of Sam's suitcase.

Usually, I had the boys set out their clothing for a trip, then I'd check and edit it and pack it for them. For some reason, Sam, then a junior in high school, packed for himself without any supervision.

Grandpa said, "Get on your suits, let's head to the beach."

Sam looked dumbstruck. "Suit? No one said anything about a suit?"

"Your bathing suit," I said.

He shrugged. "I didn't bring one."

"What did you pack?" I followed him to examine his suitcase. To my amazement he packed his Lt. Data Star Trek costume, a 24-inch flashlight and six boxes of Kraft Macaroni and Cheese.

"Why did you bring that?" I asked.

"I didn't know where we were going or what we were going to eat?"

On one hand he was oblivious, lost in his interests, but I felt a failure as his mother. The Queen of Hearts laughed, and I hugged him close so that I wouldn't hear her say, "Off with her head."

Had I been so busy that I did not follow up with him? Was I so involved with his father's transition that in trying to protect the children, I was ignoring them?

Grandpa saved the day with an extra suit, and we got through the week. The only negative comments I heard were about the length of Martin's hair. I was stuck in the middle being protective, keeping the lid on the secret, but my patience was waning.

* * *

Airline magazines are always running ads about the best steakhouses. We decided to splurge and go to a Ruth's Chris Steakhouse for dinner. Martin ordered the sixty-four-ounce porterhouse, and he always orders his steaks medium rare. They served it, and it hung over the edges of the platter. Nearly done, he pushed a couple of pieces around on his plate and told me that it was too rare to eat. I couldn't believe he ate as much as he had. When the waitress brought the bill, he balked and started a fuss about the steak which he finished. The waitress was embarrassed by the situation he put her in, his parents were embarrassed by his behavior. The boys looked at their father's empty plate and wondered why he hadn't complained if there had been a problem. I wanted out of there as quickly as possible.

That wasn't the end of it. Back home he wrote a nasty letter to the customer service department about the under-cooked meal. They responded with a form letter and a gift check for $100 off his next meal at that restaurant. He wrote back that he had no intention to ever visit that particular restaurant when he lived on the other coast. They sent another gift check for their nearest restaurant. He sashayed around proud of his accomplishment. I gave the gift certificate to Henry's girlfriend who had always wanted to eat there. He never asked about or planned to use the gift check. Probably forgotten.

* * *

During a trip to Wisconsin to visit his family, Martin suggested that we stop and pay respects to a friend. As it turned out, a friend I was unaware. He drove all of us, the kids and me, to visit this friend. We arrived at an apartment building and climbed three flights of stairs. He knocked on the door, and a large black woman answered. They embraced and chatted like old friends. The kids and I were acknowledged but never brought into the conversation or informed about how they had become friends. When we were leaving, she shook my hand and said, "So nice to meet you, Mrs. Erickson."

What the hell? Our name is not Erickson or even close to that. Why would she call me that? Who is she? Why did he bring us here? Swoop down the rabbit hole, only this time; the boys are along with me.

"Mrs. Erickson?" I said to Martin when we were alone. "Why did she call me Mrs. Erickson?"

Head down, he mumbled something. What I was to take from that was that he had identified himself as Maureen Erickson online and this friend was one of those in his circle of hypnosis. Each claiming that the other had helped them through a tough time.

It was in fact the first time they had seen each other. All this hypnosis work was online. Another example to me that he was not functioning normally. This made no sense.

If he was so good at helping others in such a manner, why the heck was he making my life a nightmare? I could sure use some hypnotherapy.

But Mrs. Erickson? As he moved forward, he needed to select a name. We discussed this one time. He told me that the female name he had chosen had been given to a family member, so he needed to find another. Then there was the last name. After I was called Mrs. Erickson, I asked him why he was using that name. Why he didn't just keep his last name. He didn't have an answer for that. Maybe he thought he shouldn't use it. I pointed out that it seemed most kept their same last name and chose a first name using the same letter as their current name. He looked contemplative.

Sometime later he told me he would take the name Maureen and keep his last name.

Goodbye Mrs. Erickson.

It took me a long time to feel comfortable to use the name Maureen. In truth I could refer to him as her or Maureen, but I avoided using her name in one-on-one conversation.

* * *

My biggest concern was how this would affect my sons. I heard their conversations knowing what I knew and could not imagine how their father's future would affect them.

There are four boys, three of them Martin's biological sons. Sam is the oldest of these three. I listened in on their conversation one day.

Sam: "I am the most like Dad."

Max: "No, I am. I am big and strong like Dad."

Sam: "Not my fault I am shorter, but I look most like Dad."

Arlo: "I am going to be most like Dad, because I get good grades."

Sam: "No, I know the most about computers and technology."

Max: "I can lift as much weight as Dad. I can lift you."

Sam: "Look at my baby picture, it looks just like Dad's."

Max: "But I look most like him now."

Sam:" No, your hair is too light. Mine is dark like his."

This type of conversation played repeatedly among the boys. They each felt that they shared at least one attribute or characteristic that marked them as most like their father. Is that how all children align themselves with their parents? How would revealing to them that their father wanted to be a woman affect them? What would happen to their role model? Where would they turn? These questions once raised, plagued me. I sought solutions before there were problems. I tried to slow Martin down.

"Can't you put this off until the boys have graduated from high school?" I pleaded. That seemed the best course of action. Give them a few more years to find their own footing. Not only would they have to deal with the reality of the situation but also that for several years they were not privy to what had been going on.

If I had to accept that he would change, then I needed him to put it off until the boys were out of school or out of the house. I couldn't even think about what our life would be like then – would we be together? How was I going to deal with that? I kept pushing those long-term issues .Trying to imagine a future for us ... together.

In honesty there was another thought. A life apart on my own terms. But knowing that he had the upper hand about our finances, I needed a strategy.

Painting White Roses Red

I laughed when the story detailed the painting of the roses. There was a rumor that they painted the grass at my high school. Rather than spend time and money perfecting the lawn, they sprayed it green.

But it was not funny as I began to notice little changes in Martin.

When Martin had chemotherapy, he lost all his hair. He sat on the bed one evening and put his hands on his scalp.

"Look," he said.

I watched as he pulled away handfuls of brown hair. His eyes showed both surprise and shock. I took his hands in mine.

"It'll grow back."

67

"Will it?"

It was not just the hair on his head, but his eyebrows and his beard. Instead of having to shave daily, he only had to shave once a week, if at all. He didn't complain about that.

"So, this is what it would feel like not to have a beard," he said, rubbing his fingers over his soft cheeks and neck.

"Is it so bad?" I asked.

"It's that my beard was so thick. It hurt to shave."

Martin's hair grew back. It came back thinner, his hairline receding, a little bare spot on the top, all within acceptable margins for his age. His eyebrows grew back, so did his beard, thick and dark as ever. He returned to shaving daily. As he regained his strength, he revisited his workout routine during lunch. He lifted weights, rode the stationary bicycle, and on weekends he rode bikes with a friend. He was getting into good shape.

He started getting massages at the gym and making other appointments. I wasn't aware of them before they happened, but I was on alert because of the results. He tried electrolysis and what I saw were red swollen cheeks from the treatment. His co-workers asked if the cancer was back because of this puffiness. He moved his appointments to after work.

"I'm trying to thin my beard out a bit. You know even if I shave first thing in the morning, I need to shave again before bed," he explained to me.

I had never known him to shave more than once in any twenty-four-hour period, but it was his face, not mine. But there were other changes.

"I ordered contacts today," he said, "colored ones."

"What colors?"

"You'll see," he said.

Later, he sat down smiling at me and instead of his deep brown eyes, there were Liz Taylor's violet ones looking back at me, or blue ones, or green ones. I felt the conspirator when he wore the blue ones to a family function, and my sister acknowledged.

"Oh, Martin, I never realized you had such beautiful blue eyes before."

* * *

Returning from a business trip, I climbed into bed and ran my hands over his chest. I liked the feel of muscle and hair. My fingers found no hair to twirl around. I pushed back and sat up.

"What happened to your chest?" I asked.

"Oh, nothing."

"No, the hair is gone."

"I was just playing around, tried a laser treatment."

"Laser?" I questioned.

"Well, the electrolysis is painful, I thought laser might be less so."

I shut my mouth. I knew the Cheshire cat was behind me, watching, ready to start with his questions. What was Martin doing? Would I dare ask? If I didn't ask, would it go away?

* * *

"I made an appointment with that company that fixes hair loss." He said. "You know, Hair Club for Men. Do you want to come along?"

I wasn't sure what the company did for hair loss, but I suspected it would be a temporary fix like a toupee. Martin made fun of his uncle for having a toupee. Would Martin wear one? The company was well appointed and made the client feel at the center of attention. They showed before and after photos and talked about the fact that with their hair product you could do all your normal activities even swim and shower. Martin signed up and was color matched and measured. There would be a three-week lag before the product was ready and they scheduled an appointment for the fitting.

He came home looking like a new man. His hair was as thick as it had been in his youth and beautifully coifed. Martin had not spent time at salons or much time in front of the mirror with his hair. He would either decide on his own or be instructed by me to get a haircut, and he would go and have it cut. Cut, not styled. Now he was styled.

The cost of the hairpiece was pricey, to say the least. A styling appointment was due every four to six weeks that cost about $60. Here was the clinker. Martin would have his hair styled on Tuesday and look great. But over the weekend he would go scuba diving, and afterward, his hair was atrocious, and he would not do anything for another five weeks. I suggested that he do his scuba diving before the hair appointment, but he did not make the connection and did not change his schedule.

We were at the beach for a family get together, and my brother-in-law was more than a little curious about Martin's hair. He was worried about his own receding hairline and little bald spot and realized Martin had done something. Martin would not tell him honestly. I felt sad that he was unwilling to share when it was evident that he had done something. He strutted around like a spoiled kid with a new toy.

* * *

The optometrist wrote a new prescription and Martin bought new frames. The ones he came home wearing were a dark teal, and he was proud to tell me that he had selected them from the women's frames. They were not overtly feminine frames, but what was he trying to do?

* * *

I was on business trips every other week, mostly gone for a day or two but sometimes as long as a week. Upon my return I would encounter questionable things. I noted them but didn't ask. I was living the "don't ask – don't tell" life. The elastic waistband of one of my skirts was totally stretched out while it had been hanging in the closet. At the back of my side of the closet there were three new dresses. Well, not new but new to me. I christened these the "ugly stepsister dresses" because they were obviously Martin's eBay purchases and hideous. One was forest green taffeta with dyed to match lace overlay. Another was a black sequined "cruise" dress that must have weighed twenty pounds.

On one occasion he was out of town and that night after the boys were tucked in, I ventured to search our closet for whatever purchases were hidden there. There were women's undergarments and prosthetic devices including a hard rubber dildo. I noted that what were still in their shipping boxes were addressed to me. All of this was inside the locked cedar closet at the back of our walk-in closet.

Like that one piece of the puzzle that suddenly makes the rest of the pieces fall into place, I had to face the fact that Martin was taking steps to become a woman; the electrolysis, the laser treatments, contacts, glasses, toupee and purchases. The whole new man wanted to be a woman.

I needed to figure out how I fit.

I would say that the woman who finds evidence that her husband is having an affair could not feel any different than I did. I was shocked and hurt. I felt that our relationship was open and honest but now I knew different. I didn't know what to do. But knew not to overreact.

With or without me, he was moving in this direction. It was the fact that he was doing this without concern for me...or the children that hurt the most. At this point I knew I needed to formulate my own plan.

My Vagina Dialog

Alice looked at herself in the mirror. She was short, blonde with shapely legs and breasts, a little too much around the middle. She thought that maybe someday she would have a tummy tuck to take her back to the shape she desired. She smiled at her reflection, but the reflection frowned back. She wondered if it was not her reflection but her conscience. She recommitted to her husband and their marriage, but she felt trapped. She allowed her fear to guide her to the safest route despite all signs indicating this way lead farther down the rabbit hole.

I urged Martin to explore his options and to meet with a counselor. I hoped that he would come to the conclusion that he was not meant to be a woman and that he would forget all this nonsense. That was my prayer so that life would return to known ground and our sons could be kept from "the knowing."

But things transpired beyond that point. We've reached a boundary to this other world and crossed over the threshold. "A little further," I told myself, "And he'll see this is not for him."

Now the children had been told; family members and friends, work peers and bosses had been told. To move forward, everyone had to be told. Yet, I clung to the thought that it could still be undone.

"If I am to be as supportive as I say I am, I need to venture out in public," I told myself. "My view of him as female is too narrow; perhaps I am wrong." This had been an internal conversation for days, weeks, months but yet I'd not taken that first step.

In the movie ***Ground Hog Day,*** Bill Murray's character is lost in time as February second repeats over and over. The only control he had was what he did that day; there were no consequences beyond that day. As he stepped off the curb into the street every morning, he stepped into a pothole of icy water that flooded his shoe and washed over his pant leg. Each day as this happened, his old high school mate, Ned Ryerson, laughed and called out, "Watch that first step, it's a doozie."

My venture out in public with Martin was just that — a doozie. Looking back, meeting in a public place for a cup of coffee and conversation, or a sandwich would have been the right thing to do. Make it a more like a blind date and let it build. No, not for me.

Martin returned from a Tuesday evening session and handed me the Polaroid of him taken after he had been dressed and styled. In that photograph, a woman posed in a floral pattern dress and a single strand of pearls with shoulder length auburn hair. Her hands were clasped in her lap, wearing a Mona Lisa smile. Her makeup had been deftly applied, and the overall effect was becoming, certainly not beautiful. I thought that Maureen resembled her cousin and a younger version of her paternal grandmother. I knew that Maureen hoped to look like her mother as a young twentyish model. The woman in the picture was not "gorgeous," but acceptable. As I returned the photo, I realized that Martin had a high opinion of himself as this woman. This was not the time for me to remind him that if he could not be a gorgeous woman, he would not become a woman.

"And this was before the facial feminization surgery," Martin said. I heard this and felt the train pulling out of the station. It's a one-way trip with no return to "normal."

The white rabbit dashed across the hallway, clutching his watch in his hand.

"A doctor is coming to discuss the surgery, and the group will all be there," Martin said. "Will you come?"

"When?"

"Saturday at three."

I didn't want to go, I didn't want to hear about the surgery, and I didn't want Martin thinking anymore about it. On the other side of the equation, I kept saying that I had to step over the boundary. How much of my fear had to do with the fact that this was all unknown?

"Okay," I said and with both feet firmly planted, and I slid down into the rabbit hole.

In my closet, I was uncertain how to dress: what to wear. Will I dress too feminine and make the male-to-female transitioners feel uncomfortable? If I dressed too male (businesslike) will it look like I was dysphoric as well? Finally, I selected a pair of black slinky slacks, open-toed pumps, and a green/black sweater set. I applied my business makeup and hoped that was right.

At the conference center, we took seats in a theatre-like setting facing a large pull-down screen. Martin's counselor, Miranda Taupe, a sixtyish psychologist who had authored a book on transsexuals was there to welcome everyone. There were nineteen men in the group. They met twice a month, and in addition to being counseled in the program, they hosted guest presenters to guide them through the more practical day-to-day business of becoming women. Topics included hair, makeup, poise, walking, conversation, dressing, hygiene, and speech.

After each of these sessions, I questioned Martin. I saw books lying around that were recommended reading; Martin's response was that it was not all that necessary, that he knew how to be a woman. I saw this outing as a chance to see Maureen in public with her circle of peers and support.

Miranda welcomed everyone and introduced Dr. Greene, the renowned surgeon who chose to specialize in male to female sexual reassignment surgery. He stood before a rapt audience of about twenty – I was the only family member of the seventeen peers in attendance. I sat next to Martin, and about half of the group were dressed as male. Some were made up as female, yet it was not hard to identify the transgendered among them.

Dr. Greene took the podium and began with the necessary housekeeping about where he performed the surgery, why he only operated in Appleton, Wisconsin, the recovery times, costs and expectations.

"There is no reason why after surgery you will not be able to achieve orgasm," he declared. This was followed by a chorus of "oohs" and "aahs" from the audiences.

I clenched my Kegel muscles and thought, "No way," protective of my natural gender, unhappy about men thinking that becoming women was easy.

The lights dimmed, and a slide show began. It started with the overview of the surgical procedure.

"Before you even board the plane, you must take care of a certain matter at home. As you will schedule your surgery about a year out – during that time you must live as a woman twenty-four-seven; change your identification, dress and act as a woman and use your female name. You must undergo electrolysis of the testicles and penis – all hair must be removed. This is critical."

He paused for effect.

I imagined the technician masked, crouching, perched over the groin with their tools removing each and every hair follicle. I thought this is way too up close and too personal.

I tuned back to the speaker.

"…Then the skin of the scrotum is removed, and again any remaining hair is removed. This skin is saved for reuse. The testes are removed and disposed. The testosterone stops here!" the surgeon said with triumph in his voice.

There was tentative applause from the audience.

Maureen moved forward expecting the next step. I continued to squirm in my seat.

"Next the skin on the penis is removed to be reused later. Again, any remaining hair must be removed. The bundle of nerves that make up the autonomic response of pleasure is refitted to become the clitoris."

There was an audible intake of air, a kind of group gulp.

"There is no cutting or change so that the orgasmic pleasure is still there."

The gulp became a whoosh that almost sounded like "Aahhhhh." Everyone was climaxing on the promise.

"The skin of the penis and the scrotum will become the vagina, labia minor and major. Throughout the surgery, there is very little blood loss and very short recovery time. You are able to get up and walk the very next day. You are moved into a ward where you are under a nurse's care while you continue your recuperation and learn to live with your new body."

The slide show changed to that of the female genitalia.

I was afraid that I might learn something about my body that I didn't already know. I was dispirited to find that changing from male to female was less strenuous and painful than doing something as natural as giving birth.

With a laser pointer, the surgeon bounced the red dot between the clitoris and the anus. "Sharp at the top and sharp at the bottom," he said moving from one slide to the next. "The reason we make you go through all that electrolysis is so that you don't end up with a hairy vagina."

There were countless slides of vaginas, and on each slide, he flicked the red laser dot punctuating the clitoris and the anus and repeated over and over, "Sharp at the top and sharp at the bottom." With each red laser dot, I jumped in my seat, as if zapped by it, slouching and straightening.

The slides changed to examples of "botched jobs."

"These were people who had their surgery done in third world countries. Of course, it costs less but there are no standards of practice, and many are done by physicians who may be doing this for the first or only time. This is my specialty; I have performed thousands…"

My mind wandered. Thousands? How many men were crossing over the gender line? What had seemed so unique and preposterous now sounded run of the mill and accepted. Mental note to self, other than Christine Jorgenson how many men had sex reassignment surgery? Were records kept? What was the success rate? Were they able to enjoy successful lives after surgery? What happened to their families?

"…Some of these people I could not help. (And in an aside) "Such a shame."

I closed my eyes after what seemed like a million vaginas had flashed before me. I thought of the Kathy Bates character in **Fried Green Tomatoes.** She was unable to bring herself to look at her own vagina with the aid of a mirror. This was beyond that, and I had all but wiggled out of my seat.

Finally, the show moved from vaginas to breasts. Dr. Greene began with how to select the right size. "Bigger is not always better," he warned.

I remembered as a teenager how I found that my breast fit perfectly into the cup of my hand and wondered if that was true for everyone. I crossed my arms under my breasts in a protective move that comforted me. My eyes stayed on the slides; I couldn't look at Martin. I could feel his enthusiasm, his expectancy, and I did not share in it.

Finally, the last slide appeared on the screen; it displayed Dr. Greene's name and address and an extensive list of contact information. I exhaled congratulating myself on making it through. I wanted to go home and hunker down in the back of my closet. I needed some alone time to digest what I witnessed.

"To schedule your surgery, you need to have lived one year as a woman, that means name change, dress as a woman, use the women's restrooms, etc. Miranda can go over this with you. You must get two independent evaluations that you are a good candidate for the reassignment surgery, and only then can you call and schedule the surgery." He announced that he is now making appointments for the coming spring.

Maureen rubbed her hands together; she wanted to race up to the podium and say, "Take me first" if she could.

Everyone moved slowly leaving the auditorium. All seventeen peers shook the hand of the surgeon and took his information packet. Several of Maureen's peers came over to meet me. I was a curiosity.

Martin introduced me to Miranda and despite myself, I liked her. I met Jessica, and I was drawn to her. Her style and dress were understated, and there was something "feminine" about her mannerisms. I measured her up and felt that she could easily pass as a woman and wished that Maureen would pay more attention so that she could carry it off too.

No, wait – I didn't want that.

There was a suggestion that the group go together to dinner. Martin looked to me, and I agreed to go, not because I wanted to, but because I was caught up in the current and lacked the strength to fight it. I was overwhelmed, overloaded, and my dream seemed beyond redemption.

At dinner, Jessica told the group about Esprit, an annual one-week event held in Washington State where transsexuals were welcome. "There are classes and a dance. The town welcomes everyone."

"Are you going?" she asked Maureen.

I held my breath.

"I didn't know about it," Maureen said. "When is it?"

"May something, middle of the month, they have a website," said Jessica.

Later there was talk at the table about scheduling surgery. Most agreed they would schedule with Dr. Greene and travel to Wisconsin when it was their time. There was some talk about the fact that the surgery in Thailand was under $10,000 instead of over $35,000.

Jessica said something to me.

'What?" I asked. I was having a hard time taking it all in and tracking conversations.

"I can never follow through," she said, "I haven't' got the money. You're lucky," she said nodding toward Maureen.

"Do you have children?" I asked.

"Yeah, a boy and girl," she told me. "The minute I told my wife, she took the kids, and I am not allowed to see them."

I was saddened, and there were others around the table that told similar stories. Not all were married, not all fathered children. In their telling, some lost brothers and sisters, mothers and fathers.

As the group broke up that evening, many of them sidled up to me and said, "Maureen is lucky," or "It's good to meet someone who is supportive." I began to feel like Mother Theresa; I could be the patron saint of transsexuals. Like the saint who stood with one foot on the head of a snake, I could stand with one foot on a discarded penis.

"What?" I've missed something again.

Miranda was standing next to me and asked, "Does he let you know how much he loves you?"

I thought, "Are you kidding?" but said, "No." I answered truthfully without considering what I was saying or who I was saying it to. Could I say something that got him thrown out of the program and marked as "unfit for reassignment"? Would I say it if there was?

"We'll work on that," she told me.

Later I thought about this. She was not the first person to tell me this, that he loved me so, or spoke highly of me. To me, he was condescending and critical. He was not complimentary or thoughtful. Why was this? Was it in response to some inner turmoil that he cannot handle? Does it build to a point where it spilled over and got redirected at me?

Sitting through the surgery talk was pushing me into discomfort. It also gave me an opportunity to meet the counselor and Martin's trans peers. Despite my prejudices, I liked them, and a certain amount of empathy came into play for how many of them had been treated by their partners.

At the same time, I was beginning to realize that all the empathy in the world wouldn't make Martin be the partner I needed as we moved forward.

Getting Ready to Tell

Ten years passed between our conversation early Christmas Day in the closet and when the telling began. He had sworn me to secrecy – not to tell my sisters, my friends — anyone. I was the dutiful wife, true to him. But the secrecy took its toll on me. I held back not to give something away; appeared cheerful when I was scared. I remember feeling that the life he wanted to embark on was one of back street alleys and among the disenfranchised. I was more mainstream and always wanting to fit in.

Our sex life was the same as it had been. There was no change, but I could feel myself walking the tightrope, wanting what had been, afraid of what would be ahead.

Those ten years passed quickly in retrospect. At the time, I was busy, and unless we were alone and the subject was being discussed, it hung in the air — life went on as it had.

At some point, I crossed over the boundary and knew that the gender change would be a reality, not just his dream anymore. Right or wrong he would make the change because he was fixated on it. I began to turn my full attention to my sons. I wanted them to have a healthy relationship with their father but was concerned that they understood that this was their father's choice, and that they were not responsible for what would happen next.

One day I was keeping Martin's secret and trying to insulate him, then I was not. I was not out to embarrass or harm him. My allegiance was now wholly with the children.

We would have to break the silence. We would have to tell. From my trans family friends, I got advice. We would need to tell the children first, and before we told them, we would want to select a counselor who could help them understand; a neutral party that would be available to answer their questions. I made a list of gender dysphoric counselors and consulted with Martin so that together we would interview them and select one that had not spent time already with either of us. Imagine how many there were on that list? He had already met at least two of them, and I had met with one. That took three off the list immediately.

The one we selected was perfect. A calm female who was up to the task of working with youngsters who would have to accept that their parent would be changing, still their parent, but certainly not to continue looking the same. It was hard enough to be a teenage boy but to also deal with your male role model becoming female was unconscionable to me. I was terrified for my sons. I redirected this terror toward education and understanding. We were headed into unchartered territories.

Martin still carried angst over his own parents' divorce when he was a teen. I did not want that for my sons.

There is a rule book. The curriculum has you live as a woman for a full year before you can schedule surgery. During this time, you must come out to family, friends, co-workers and use your feminine name and dress, and act as a woman at all times. You apply for a new birth certificate, driver's license, social security card, passport, Costco card, and library card. One day you are Martin, then you are Maureen.

He received an invitation to his high school reunion and went online and had his contact info changed from Martin to Maureen. It was the ease at which he could do this that alarmed me, and the fact that he did not consider how this change, unexplained, would be received by those he wanted to reconnect with. That little fact, the one that he seemed oblivious to how anyone would react, caused me concern. Was he so caught up in himself that he did not see that some finesse might be needed, or did he not care what anyone thought?

Martin and the white rabbit were on an overzealous schedule that would leave our family in ruins. Next, we had to sort how we would tell other members of the family. Martin had his mother, father, stepmother, brother and cousins. There were uncles and aunts, and there would be his employer and peers as well. I would have my sisters to tell; my parents were already deceased. I couldn't begin to imagine how my father might have responded.

More than making a list and prioritizing who we would tell and when, we also had to consider how people would respond and what steps we might have to take to maintain relationships. Hardest of all would be telling Martin's father.

For me, accepting that this was not going to be derailed was the hardest step. I began to talk myself off the edge and to calm down and accept that this change would happen. I could not let go of my hope for it all to be gone nor my anger over the changes thrust upon me.

Cracks in Silence

Summertime and the boys were out of school. Sam would be a senior, Max and Arlo would be entering eighth grade. They were debating the advantages and disadvantages of the new Xbox, and PlayStation video consoles. They argued the pros and cons of each and asked me for one or the other when we intersected. Meanwhile, I was looking at eleven hundred square feet of redwood deck that needed to be stained.

"I've got an idea," I said at breakfast.

"Oh no," mumbled Sam.

"What?" asked Arlo?

"I'll buy you the game console of your choice..."

"PlayStation," said Sam, lurching forward.

"Xbox," said Arlo, elbowing Sam.

"I don't care, I just want the new Mario," said Max.

"What's the catch, Mom?" Sam asked.

"I'll buy you the game console of YOUR choice in payment for you refinishing the deck," I said.

"Xbox or PlayStation?" asked Arlo

"Exactly!" I said. "You have to pick. And all agree."

"Oh." They said in unison.

"What do we have to do to the deck?" Max asked.

"You'll need to remove everything from the deck..."

"Ugh," groaned Sam.

"...and use a pressure washer to clean it. There are a lot of loose nails, and I want those removed, and deck screws put in..."

"Too much work," said Sam.

"And two games?" negotiated Arlo.

"...then stain it," I finished.

"Okay," said Max.

The boys continued their discussion over game consoles. They were occupied for a couple of weeks. I rented the pressure washer and bought the stain, deck screws, and paintbrushes. They got to work. It took a day to take the plants and furniture off the deck. Then they swept it. Day two we turned on the power washer and worked to remove the dirt and grime, but not to erode the wood grain. There was a lot of supervision on day two. On Monday, when I returned to work, they were laying on skateboards, pulling up the loose nails and using the power drill to put in the deck screws. It seemed like they were moving along quickly, but that was the scene for the whole week.

For the past six months, Martin had been painting his toenails a bright blood red. He agreed to keep socks on whenever he was out of our bedroom. Like a young woman with budding breasts, there was a growing desire to strut her stuff. He walked out onto the deck barefoot while the boys were working.

Without looking at the black hairs on his toes and shins, one of the boys asked a question of Mom and was surprised by Dad's voice in response. He laid the screwdriver down and looked up to see his father standing over him.

He looked down again at the toenails and asked, "How come your toenails are painted?"

Was that the last innocent question he would ask? So many things could have happened next, but the hormonal teenage girl lied shamelessly.

"Mom did it," Martin said.

"Why?" he asked.

"She was just having fun," he said.

"Oh," was his response as he picked up the screwdriver and continued earning his game console.

Later that day one of my other sons asked me, "Did you paint Dad's toenails?"

I was unaware of what had transpired on the deck earlier. I could have kept the lid on the pressure cooker, but like a pressure cooker I was getting too close to the "she's going to blow" setting.

"No," I said. "Why?"

"Dad said you did for fun," he said.

"Oh." This time it was my turn. Head down I concentrated on making dinner. Out of the corner of my eye, I saw the white rabbit scamper across the kitchen muttering "I'm late. I'm soooooo late." I waited for what was to come.

I chopped a lot of vegetables and fruits during those years. My frustration at feeling out of control fueled my anger. Fear kept that anger at a slow burn. Unwilling to unleash that anger at him, I used it to make everything else work. How to get ahead at work, how to outsell the competition ... how to keep the kids safe, myself projecting sanity. And always with a prayer that this thing would go away.

Coming Out

The white rabbit stops and checks his watch again. He flicks the timepiece and shakes it. He holds it up to his ear and listens. He shrugs his shoulders, redeposits the watch into the pocket and hops off.

"I sent the letter to my mom," Martin told me.

"I didn't know that you had written it," I said. I am shocked and dismayed. I thought we had a plan; I thought we would tell the boys first. Now he's on some alternate plan.

"Yeah, I worked on it last night and mailed it today."

"What about your Dad?"

"Well, that's going to be harder. But I told Mom."

The proverbial cat was now out of the bag. The telling had begun. Martin started with his mom and then told his brother. He developed a very predatory habit of lying in wait on Yahoo messenger and when he saw your status as "online," he would pounce with a "Hi," and start a conversation. I had deleted Yahoo Messenger from my computer at work because of this. I blamed the deletion on the Network Administrator, but as a Vice President, he knew that I could overrule it.

His younger brother, Mark, on hearing (or reading online) was at a loss. He told his wife who was a teacher, and together they began their own internet research. Mark was a practicing Jew and a lawyer like his father and uncles, whereas Martin had always been off on his own path.

Martin intercepted his cousin, Sandra, and had a long online conversation telling her. She was accepting and receptive, and they became much closer.

The pattern began to emerge that those who were embracing the change were held close; those that were standoffish or downright against it were ignored. He contacted peers he had worked closely with, invited them to lunch and told them. He had mixed reactions. Most reacted with shock.

"What does Alice have to say about this?" they asked.

After work, he would tell me who he had come out to and how they reacted. When he told his cousin,

Gary, and Aunt Rosemary who had been close to our family, their reaction was the same, "What does Alice have to say about this?"

"This isn't about you; this is about me. Why does everyone ask that?" He related to me with despair.

That was upsetting for me to hear. More difficult was the actual digestion of what it meant. I had little or no bearing on his life. I was not a crucial centerpiece to his life, but a character in a supporting role. I began to feel this, but it would not sink in for some time yet.

After telling so many people, I wondered what his plan was. We still hadn't told the boys. His fear was telling his father. He told his brother in hopes that he would tell their father for him. If not tell him, at least set the scene. Martin feared that his father would not be supportive and that he would be ostracized from the family. There was some history that would support this.

Finally, Martin lit on the plan to tell his stepmother and ask her to tell his father. In the back of his mind, he formulated a plan that if his father did not accept his change, he would remove his access to our children, his grandchildren.

He did not tell me this at the time, but it would play out and become the division between us. I refused to deny the boys access to their only living grandparents. This was not about them; it was about Martin. His single-minded selfishness appalled me.

We agreed to take the boys and visit his parents for Thanksgiving. One last family Thanksgiving was how I thought of it. After that, we would tell the boys. That was our plan.

Between the time that we planned the Thanksgiving trip and the actual journey, Martin had come out to his brother, his cousins, his aunt, his stepmother, and several work peers. I felt I needed a score card to know who knew and who did not. Our communication seemed nonexistent. We might converse about household topics, but any genuine exchange of feelings was gone. I no longer trusted him to tell me the truth, too many times what he said was not reflected in how he acted. The fact that he had started this "telling" before we had agreed to do it, let me know that he was working to his own timetable. The boys still did not know.

The boys enjoyed their visit with Grandpa and Grandma. We had a huge Thanksgiving dinner. Behind closed doors, Martin and Mark whispered. Martin's stepmother and I shared thoughts. Martin tried to coerce his stepmother to tell his father so that he would not have to.

She said that she could not, but that she would be as supportive as she could.

Martin did not take the opportunity to sit down with his father and try to explain while we were there. And it only got harder when we got home.

97

I saw the question in their eyes, "What was Martin thinking?" Mark asked me if I thought he was taking drugs or being influenced by someone or something. He raised his doubts to me, not Martin.

Family History: Martin's father was the eldest of four brothers; the third brother was the black sheep. He had fathered five children, was divorced, and lived with their mother. He was unable to hold down a job and was considered eccentric. I heard all kinds of strange stories about his behavior but only met him once. He was the odd little man who stood out in the crowd in his checkered vest, suit jacket, and obviously mismatched toupee. The toupee of black hair sat atop his longer graying hair.

He was involved in an automobile accident and when taken by ambulance was found to be wearing women's underwear. Later, when his brothers cleared his belongings from their mother's house, they found an obscene amount of pornography and the uncles whispered among themselves, but I was never privy to what they knew. Was he also transgendered? Is there something in the DNA or genetic history that would affect Martin? Would it reappear in my sons?

Often things don't get better when you avoid the confrontation. Martin didn't tell his father. But he told his cousins, and they spoke of it to their fathers. They in turn sought their older brother, Martin's father, and asked what he thought of it. He had no clue what they were talking about.

Ultimately he was angry that his own son could not share this big as life problem with him. He declined to meet Maureen saying that he would rather remember his son, Martin.

The following year, he was diagnosed with pancreatic cancer and given no more than three month to live. Maureen tried again to get her father to meet her and again was refused.

Meanwhile I traveled with the boys to say our goodbyes, and he was gone within that first month. Maureen regretted that she had not worked out a reconciliation but traipsed into the funeral. I say traipsed because the stories I heard was that she made it all about her and not honoring her father.

Again, I found myself in the middle. My former father-in-law was someone I cared about. He was grandfather to my children now at his life's end. Maureen was unable to connect with her father because of her transition. I was stronger by then and firmer with her that I would not tolerate the threat that she wanted to make denying the children from their grandparents. Much to Maureen's dismay I took them to his deathbed.

Letting Go of My Silence

I am the oldest of seven sisters, and with the passing of our parents, we tried to get together once a year and spend a few days, just the sisters without husbands or children. We planned to meet in Arizona in January. I vacillated about going or not. Not everyone could go this time, so I had an out. I knew that if I went, I needed to break my silence. But something was holding me back. If I opened up about it, there was no going back. My sisters would know and not let me hide. All my life I had been a planner; if I do this, then that. I could see far beyond the horizon, but in this, I was stuck in the present and unwilling to peer forward. I knew that there could be no future for us, but that was not what I wanted.

101

I believed that if I revealed what Martin wanted to do, he would move forward, and the boys and I would not. It wasn't that I was unwilling, it was that I knew somewhere in that secret inside place, that he wanted to be free of us to pursue his dreams. As long as I hid this truth, as long as I stayed in this place, there was the possibility that it could be undone.

"Well, I had the worst nightmare, ever," he might say.

"What was that?" I'd ask.

"I dreamed I wanted to be a woman."

"What? That's the stupidest thing ever. You? A woman? Impossible."

"I know," he'd say. "And what about my cock? Absurd."

Just like Bobby Ewing in the shower at that end of season "Dallas," everything would be back to normal. We'd know, but no one else would. Safety.

But also in that secret place, I knew that was not going to happen, so I booked my flight and joined my sisters. I was ready to tell, to move forward, and reclaim my sanity.

Out of the seven of us, only four were able to get away — the two oldest and the two youngest. Each took their turn bringing the others up to date on their lives; I sat silent.

After so many years of silence, I found it harder to let it out. I didn't know where to begin.

The afternoon was growing long; soon we'd break for dinner then a movie. Would there be another time to talk like this? Another time we would all be together?

"There is something I have to tell you," I blurted.

"What?" they asked in unison. Their eyes turned to me, and I burst into tears.

Cathy hugged me and said, "Tell us."

When I couldn't talk, she said, "It's alright whatever it is, I have never seen my big sister cry. What is it?"

Somehow, I found the words and told them that my husband wanted to be a woman and was taking hormones and planned to have surgery. I could have told them that I have two heads or started talking in tongues. They seemed prepared for anything. In confiding to them, I moved to another place. Their hugs and words of support were powerful. They showered me with compassion, but their underlying message was that I had to get out of there. They each said that they would contact one of the missing sisters and bring them up to date. Their messages were less compassionate.

Rachel called me the day after I got home. She called me at the office — not at home — and said that Cathy had told her. "Oh Alice," I only have one word for you "RUN." I know you have all this sense of loyalty and compassion blah blah blah, but you need to RUN girl."

Polly and I walked five miles together every Friday. I planned to tell her when we walked next. She had questions about the sisters' weekend she had missed, and I didn't get around to my big news until we were into mile two. Polly was the meek and compassionate one of us. She gritted her teeth together and stopped mid stride.

"Alice, I am sorry but all I can see is that he is selfish. He is not thinking about the boys or you." She spared no feeling for him. I was a bit surprised by this but realized that I was too close to the issue. Despite this difference of opinion, we continued our walks every Friday, and I owe it to her that I softened my grip on making it easy for him and asked more for what I needed.

Darla lived out of state and had gone through a divorce in the five months between the deaths of our father and mother. She called me crying and wanting to know what was going on. We talked: her troubles were financial, but she thought mine were worse.

Martin asked me what my sisters had to say. My allegiance had shifted. Now that they knew, their support was mine, and I told him little of what was actually said.

Before that weekend, despite the gulf that existed between us, we still shared the same bed. Martin had never been a cuddler, each of us slept enveloped in a separate comforter.

Rachel asked me, "You're not still sleeping with him, are you?"

I felt slapped silly. What had I been thinking? Why wasn't I distancing myself further? Why was I still acting like everything was going to be okay? I moved to sleeping on the couch in the living room. I don't know if the boys knew I did this, I was the first one up and usually the last one to bed. Martin never addressed this change of venue with me.

My sisters are my greatest support team. Unburdening to them moved me off my teetering balance beam and landed me on solid ground once again. The steps that followed brought more tears and more anger but now the anger was squarely at him and frustration with me and my doddering.

The Games He Played

Naïve me. After so much time, things began to come together for me. Martin spent a lot of his time online. I didn't know if he was doing research or communicating because if I entered the room, the laptop was slammed shut. That was our fine line – he didn't share with me what he was doing, and I didn't want him to do what he wanted to do.

He did confide in me about who he was talking to after one incident.

"I can't believe how silly men are," he said.

"What are you talking about?"

"Oh, I posted myself as Maureen online and said I was looking to meet men."

"You did what?" At this point, he was still very much Martin, no hormones, no counseling.

"I thought it would be fun. I can't believe what they are willing to do because I tell them to."

"That's wrong," I said.

He shrugged it off. "I thought you would find it funny," he said.

I never asked what he asked them to do or if he continued or not. What happened next kicked up the craziness one notch.

It was common for us to do the errands and grocery shopping together on the weekend. We were out, when he suddenly cried, "I have to be home in ten minutes."

"Ten minutes?" I calculated we were halfway through our shopping, and it was at least a ten-minute drive home. "Why?"

"My mistress…"

"What? Who?" I stood staring at him. What was he talking to me about. *His mistress?*

The grocery aisle scene swirled around, and I dropped down into the rabbit hole or did I rise out of it?

He stammered and stuttered and said he had to go home, and he had to go now.

How could some unknown entity that he communicated with online have any hold on him? That was illogical.

"No, we are going to finish our shopping and then go home," I said. I was the adult, the logical one, and mad that it was to be my role. He pouted.

When we arrived home, he bolted from the car into the bedroom and went online. He left me alone to unload the groceries and put things away.

I tried to have further conversations about the mistress and what that was all about, but he was furtive. Later these sessions turned into what he called hypnosis. It made no sense to me. He was living in an alternative reality online where he had a mistress he had to obey and subjects that relied upon him to hypnotize them. Words on a screen? Hypnosis? And now he had brought us into this alternate reality.

The mad hatter seemed saner than Martin or Maureen or whoever.

He included me as a party to whatever oddity the boys witnessed as he did about going barefoot on the deck. Never knowing what blame he put on me created a quandary.

I was keeping his secret but he was using my name for his own purpose — putting me in harm's way. He was using me to get what he wanted. I could feel that we were no longer working to the same goals. I began to realize that a future together was less likely.

Telling the Boys

Children pick up the clues dropped by their parents, and if our sons contemplated what was going on, they did not confide.

I tried to bring issues of transgender into their awareness. There seemed to be a lot of it when you were looking for it. A new television show started that year staring Richard Dreyfuss, **The Education of Max Bickford.** He played a college professor who had discontinued his relationship with a longtime friend after that friend transitioned from male to female.

I waited for this show to start and then encouraged my children to sit and watch with me. It was before we told them and I wanted to see if they had questions or comments, but this was a minor subplot of the series.

What we did watch was the first season of American Idol and we sat taking in every nuance of that first season and cheering on who we thought was the best.

Years later they would have to deal with Chandler Bing's trans father on **Friends.**

Their reaction when we told them was caution, not outrage. There were a couple of incidents that occurred before we sat them down to tell them that may have prepared them. In the end, I believe they suspected that we would tell them that we were divorcing. They told me later that is what they expected.

* * *

On Tuesday evenings, Martin was attending his counseling courses. He would go after work and often stopped at a salon to be dressed and have hair and makeup done. He agreed to come home as Martin. I tried to be home, but one night I had a meeting. This time he called ahead and told the son who answered the phone that he needed a favor. He asked them to unlock the slider to the master bedroom and leave it unlocked.

Our oldest son, Henry, took the call and watched for what would happen. He thought it odd that his father called and asked this. He heard his father's car and watched a woman run across the lawn and through the side gate to the master bedroom. He thought his father was having an affair.

Imagine how he lay in bed that night worrying over this.

One of my online trans family friends had struck a similar arrangement with her husband. When he went out, he left as him and returned as her. She negotiated with him that when he returned, he was to honk as he arrived, she would go into the study and stay there until he had come in, showered and changed. She did not participate in his dressing, but like Martin, her husband planned to make the transition to female. They were both in their sixties, and I worried for how she would deal with this.

Another trans family friend was at the time asking for guidance; her husband was scheduled for surgery in the coming week, and she feared for his health and her sanity.

I read their mail and considered how to support them, always conscious that the secrecy kept me from my local support. I hoped that if I kept the secret, it could go away, and no one (our family or friends) would be the wiser. It would be like hitting the "undo" button, and life could resume.

* * *

The next event was more traumatic. Martin had the habit of holing up in the bedroom after work. I catered to him — brought him his dinner and didn't return till I had done the dishes, helped the boys with homework, baths, laundry, and bedtime. When everyone was settled down, I entered the bedroom and got ready for bed. He was usually at the desk on his laptop and/or watching television. That night as I climbed into bed, two doors opened simultaneously. Max opened the door to the bedroom to give his parents a hug before bed, and Martin pulled open the door from the dressing area wearing my aqua nightgown.

Max's eyes dilated with surprise, then shock. He turned in confusion and raced up the stairs. I was out of bed and behind him all the way. I sat down on his bed as he heaved tears into his pillow.

"Max," I said, "let me explain."

Then Martin was there in the room, He had put on his bathrobe.

I turned to him, "Go."

"Is Dad gay?" Max asked when the tears subsided.

"No," I said. "I am sorry he scared you." I wanted to blurt out everything but knew that in doing so, it might calm me, but it would not belay his fears. Better for me to keep mum a little longer.

When he was settled and quiet, I retreated to our bedroom.

"What were you thinking?" I demanded.

"I thought you would like it?"

I took my pillow and comforter and went into the living room and slept on the couch. I did not want the boys to find me there, but I needed distance from Martin. It was time to bring everything out into the open.

* * *

I told the boys that we would be having a family dinner Saturday night and I wanted them all there; only Henry, the oldest was not living at home. That night their Dad sat at the head of the table. I told them that he had something to tell them and let him speak. There was no histrionics, no drama.

He quietly explained that ever since he was small, he had felt confused about his identity and felt that he was a girl inside, and not a boy.

"When I would watch the *Mickey Mouse Club* on TV, I watched the girls. I wanted to be like them," he said.

He explained that sometimes this happens and that there is a way that this can be corrected and that he is seeing a counselor and is making plans to become a woman. He discussed that soon he will have to spend a year dressing and acting as a woman. He told them that he will change his name from Martin to Maureen.

They listened and asked few questions. Each pair of eyes turned from their Dad to me with one burning question.

"How does this affect me?" they wanted to ask.

But what they did ask was, "Mom what do you think about all of this?

"We still love each other and are not planning to divorce. Your Dad must do what he has to do. He has been plagued with depression for years, and if this makes the difference in his life, he must do it."

That's what I said and what I believed, or at least wanted to believe. I was clinging to the hope that this little change — from male to female — would correct everything that was wrong and everything that was right would not be disturbed. I also believed in Santa Claus and the Easter Bunny and Happily Ever After endings.

There was a large Costco-sized bag of pretzels in the pantry, and when I entered the kitchen the next morning, I could see that there were bits and pieces on the counter. Before I swept them into the garbage, I looked down. The bits and pieces spelled out "We Love You." This was the message my sons left.

There comes a moment when a parent sees that the values they wanted to pass on to their children have been received. Either they were willing to accept this for their father's sake or they were clinging to the same belief in Happily Ever After as their mother.

Their father told them he would always be their father, and that he loved them, but in public now they were not to call him "Dad."

They came to me with their questions.

"What are we supposed to call him?"

"Are we supposed to call him Mom?"

"What do we tell our friends?"

"Do we have to tell our friends?"

"Do Grandpa and Grandma know?"

We had the open-door house where kids were always welcome and even when we took family outings it was not unusual to have one extra along for the trip. Now the kids didn't want their friends coming to the house. The kids usually found a way to word things so that no name was needed when they conversed with their father. As their father was Martin and soon would be Maureen, I suggested we call her "M" and then "Auntie M" which made me laugh. To be honest, it took me quite a while to be able to call her Maureen.

Right after that dinner, Martin excused himself to the bedroom. After a couple of moments there was a yell from the bedroom. When I went to find out what happened, Martin was on the floor by the bed. He had slipped on papers he'd left on the floor and yelled at me for not being there when he fell.

He was not concerned about how his sons took the news or wanting to sit down with them one on one and talk about it.

Braving a New World

If I were going to come out, I would tell my family members in person. I would enlist their help in telling other family members. I would invite my closest friends to lunch or dinner or out for a drink, and one by one I would share with them. I would help them cross the void to understanding. It would be necessary for me to bridge the gap and keep their friendship and support. But this isn't about my coming out.

After Martin wrote the letter to his mother, talked online with his brother, his cousins and finally his stepmother; he boldly went through his list of friends and peers. Sometimes he did it one on one over lunch, but sometimes he did it in a way that shocked and surprised.

117

I had a busy delivery day of gift baskets, and he offered to come along and help. I wasn't sure if he wanted to help or wanted me to entertain him, but I agreed. He was to meet me at the shop around ten. I got there early and took care of setting the day's priorities and loaded up my van. When I heard the clop-clop of his shoes on the linoleum floor, I turned in my chair to see that he had come in a skirt, blouse, and wig. My employees had no idea of any of this and the two, Louanne and Tina, stood gape-mouthed at my husband. I told him to get in the van and that I would be right there. I put my arms around my shocked employees, and said, "So now you know my secret. My husband wants to be a woman."

They hugged me telling me they loved and would support me. I apologized for the shock and told them I had no idea he would show up dressed like that today.

"What are you doing? I asked him as I climbed in the car.

"What?"

"Dressing like this in front of my employees? They didn't know."

"Well, I need to practice going out in public. That's why I wanted to come along today."

"But you should have told me. I could have prepared them."

I am shocked and hurt by his dismissal of other's feelings. I am worried and think that now I have to be sure to keep him out of view of any of my clients. He may have on women's clothing, but he does not pass as a woman.

"Jan called today and asked us over for dinner Saturday," Martin said.

"Sounds good," I said.

"We might be able to do another deal. She has some contracting work for me."

"What time and should I bring something?" I asked.

"She said six and no; she'll take care of everything."

As we dressed to go, I saw that he was dressing as Maureen in a black skirt and blouse. It was one of his best outfits; complimentary without being overdressed. He asked to borrow my pearls.

In the car, I asked, "What did Jan say when you told her?"

"Oh, not much."

"Did you tell her?"

"Yeah, I think so."

Oh no. This felt like a massive faux pas. We arrived at her home in an upscale neighborhood. She greeted us at the door, and the shocked look on her face clued me in that she had not been told. She was gracious, and I got my husband to explain why he was dressed that way. Jan and her husband nodded and listened, but I could hear their clocks ticking to draw the evening to a close.

Martin and I frequented a family-run Chinese restaurant for its proximity to work. We had lunch there often, and we took the boys there for dinner on many Saturday nights. We each had our favorite dishes and did take out or eat in almost every week. The waitresses knew us by name. One day, Martin called and suggested I meet him there for lunch. He arrived in dress and makeup as Maureen. Our waitress looked from him to me and back and made a joke. I was ashamed of having to play such a trick on her.

* * *

One day as I cleaned up the kitchen, Maureen clomped out of the bedroom and headed past me. It was before noon, and she was dressed in a short black velour dress cut low in the front. As usual she wore her flat black shoes which she could not walk in without making a clomp clomp sound. I don't know if it was because they were cheap shoes or she bought them without trying them on, so they didn't really fit.

I said, "You're not wearing that." It was more of an exclamation of surprise.

She pouted and said, "Why not?"

"It's inappropriate for the time of day." That was the nicest way I could object.

She stuck out her lower lip and stomped her right foot three times, then turned and fled back into the bedroom. It was the stereotypical reaction of a thirteen-year-old girl. I stood in shock and was sucked right down into the rabbit hole.

Or was I already there?

* * *

Martin kept whining that he wanted to dress up and go out as Maureen but didn't do it. One day I told him that flights to Las Vegas were cheap and hotel rooms even cheaper. Why not run to Vegas for three days, and he could go as Maureen. He said "yes." I booked the flights and hotel, and we were off. But he was too afraid, so he went as Martin and pouted about it the whole time.

I was in a tight place and beginning to realize that I was stuck in a no-win situation. Wishing it was no-whine.

I was damned if I didn't help him and damned when I did. Like the parents of a teen, you feel that you can't do anything right. I didn't want to be her parent, I tried to avoid that role but kept finding myself backed into it. I was the one he entrusted to make decisions for him; I was the one he sought when he was afraid, I was the one blamed when things didn't go the way he wanted. I heard the clock ticking off the year he should be acting as a woman, yet he was hiding in this in-between place.

* * *

Several months later when all documents identified him as Maureen, we planned to attend Esprit, the annual convention for transsexuals, transvestites, and crossdressers. It was held in Port Angeles, Washington, and for a reasonable fee, you could attend. Of course, you would meet others like you and have an opportunity to learn skills.

At this point, it seems to me that I began to be the driver. I was tired of taking a back seat, being surprised, and having the rug pulled out from under me. I was fed up with this in-between state. If you were going to become a woman, get over the awkwardness and get on with it. I didn't know if we would be able to stay together or not, but if we could, we needed to move forward. If not, we needed to hit that wall.

The problem was that I was no longer the wife but had been pushed into the mother role; the one I did not want. I knew that if I were pushed here, that would be the end of us. Maybe that is why he chose me in the first place, to take the lead and get this done for him. I'll never know, but I was working my way toward the light at the end of the tunnel – wherever the tunnel came out.

If he was going to move forward, he needed to do so. He was limited now to going to Carla's Salon twice a month where he paid to be made up, dressed up. and coifed. There he interfaced with his peers in an instruction session, that wasn't even getting close to the real world. An opportunity to go to this convention would be a good next step. I scheduled flights, hotels, and a rental car. We would be there for four days. I hadn't thought about my role while there, but several things happened that proved to be beneficial to me.

First, I had an opportunity to brush elbows with a lot of other trans people, and even more than that; I could meet with and discuss things with their spouses. Like the trans family online group, there was much that we shared. We cared about our spouses and wanted what was best for them. We were unsure what was best for us or what the future would look like.

One young couple made an impression on me. They were in their early twenties, and he was as cute as she. He was dressed as female, wearing a short mini skirt. He had grown out his hair to shoulder length, and he and his wife had a six-month-old son with them.

"We knew we wanted to have a child," she said. "We got pregnant as soon as we could because we knew he would be having the surgery right after that."

I wondered what lifestyle that little boy would grow up in. I wondered if the relationship would hold together for them.

I thought a lot during that trip about the difference between the first time he said to me that he wanted to dress in women's clothes and what I knew about the trans world today. It had been ten years. In that decade, it had moved from out of the dark corners into the shadows. For the next decade, the issue of transgender would come to primetime television, and in the following decade, Bruce Jenner would bring it to the cover of Vanity magazine.

Wives attending the Esprit convention were given a treat. A psychologist was brought in to discuss topics with them two of the four afternoons.

The trans community attended seminars about make-up, clothing selections, walking, poise, speaking and other topics. I left Martin to attend that, and I sat in on the spouse sessions.

What a relief that was. I remember one discussion where a wife complained that her spouse lay back on the bed and said to her, "Do me." She was advised that she did not have to do anything. She had every right to discuss what was acceptable and what was not. At the time, that poor woman was lost, those words opened the door for her to new behavior.

Some wives said that they had reached an agreement with their crossdressing husbands that they pursued this separate from them. One said that she and her husband enjoyed cross-dressing play for years when suddenly he wanted to become a woman and was moving away from her to do so.

Another couple I recall was older, maybe in their late sixties. He was an engineer and worked for Boeing. He felt that he had the right to choose who he was each day. If he wanted to be Ralph, he would come to work dressed as male, but again, he might choose to be Diane. In that case, he came dressed as a woman. He did this switch at the convention as well. He did not understand why this fluidity was upsetting to his co-workers or his wife. He had been given an ultimatum at work to be one or the other; too much work time was spent figuring out how to work with his persona. His wife sat quiet as a mouse, and when I watched her, I knew she was as fragile as my grandmother's hundred-year-old China. My heart went out to her.

I turned inward and asked myself what I was doing still straddling the fence.

* * *

As we were travelling to Port Angeles, I planned to have dinner with my sister who lived in Seattle and for her to meet Maureen. She made it clear that she needed to meet her without her daughter present at first. She and her husband were kind and supportive, Martin presented as Maureen, and we had a pleasant evening.

Reflecting back to this dinner, Maureen was pre-op, starting to dress in public and paid close attention to the details of hair and makeup. Her hair was too thin on top, so she wore a wig. I helped her dye her hair to match the wig and to pull her hair through the mesh cap to blend in with the wig. She wore flats to diminish her height and carried a purse. While she presented acceptable, she was not the gorgeous woman she had wanted to be, but she never commented on this to me.

* * *

There were a couple of times that we went shopping together. I helped her pick out clothing even several outfits for work, but she didn't ever actually work as Maureen. The company she was at, shuttered shortly after she came out to them. She didn't go on interviews after that.

Despite all this, I never saw her use the skills she had been shown to dress and take care to present well as a female. She relied on everything working out for her through the surgeries; first a facial feminization surgery, then the gender reassignment, then an operation where they were to alter her voice to be more feminine. And the hormones.

All of those things were aids, but they did not complete the transformation.

I saw the white rabbit check his timepiece and tap his foot impatiently. Martin seemed to be moving forward without completing all the tasks.

Stages of Grief

Shock and Denial. When he said to me that he wanted to dress in women's clothing, I was shocked. I felt that my normal life was being pulled away, replaced with some X-rated seamy side. I knew nothing about trans- anything, and I did not want to know. Over time, I learned that if I didn't say anything further about this, he did not raise the issue either. Therefore, it was forgotten, over.

Only it wasn't forgotten. Or over. I was on the lookout for any sign that he was still pursuing this. When I found evidence, I would begin the shock, hurt, and denial phase over, and over again.

At all times, I was angry that this was happening to me, to my family, to my perfect life. I was a successful negotiator and bargaining was the only logical step. I had to get him to take back and give up this dream; I had to fight for what I wanted and what I thought was right for the children. The last gambit I had was for him to wait for the boys to be out of high school. At least they would be beyond puberty.

Did I suffer depression? I certainly saw him suffer through it. I became detached from my own wants and let my concern for his well-being surpass my needs. Perhaps he knew what was right for him better than I did? And I moved into acceptance.

No one step is whole unto itself. There were bargaining and acceptance. "Let's see if he could be the woman he desires. If not, he will drop the whole thing." And with my acceptance that he had chosen this path and was not to be deterred, came more anger. This anger was aimed at his lack of concern or compassion for us, his family, present, and witnessing. My alarm was daily over what he said, what he did, or what he wore.

There were external forces as well. To that point I had been fortunate to have a great work life, or to have a balanced personal and work life. Often both were in the plus column, but if my personal life was off, I could plunge into my work life. When I had a particularly challenging boss or situation at work, home life was a pleasure. That was true until Martin wanted to be a woman. When the words finally flew from his mouth, I was caught up in a miserable situation at work that paralleled it. In fact, while Martin was taking Prozac and self-medicating so was my boss who had been my friend long before we began working together. She had a history of zeroing in on one of her employees and with laser beam precision making their life miserable. I had witnessed this many times and saw it usually blow over; it depended on several factions. Often, the target simply left the company.

She turned on me one day, and the hostility at work combined with the ever-changing landscape at home put me into the crosshairs. All the road signs pointed to exit. I had never left one job without already possessing a written offer to a new one. The economy was such there weren't many options available. To be honest, my psyche was too bruised to pump myself up to seek another job.

At any moment, I would be plotting my resignation at work, but moments later, I would rationalize that I would do better to stay in the job, tough it out, and end my marriage.

I had come to realize that I was no longer in love with my husband, I cared about him, but I was unsure who he was going to be in the end. What I witnessed in self-centeredness, and what I could only name as a disregard for the feelings of his family, pushed me away.

One morning I came out of the shower, and he tried to lure me back into bed. There was the feeling that I should give in to his request, but I could not bring myself to do so.

"No," I said.

"Don't you love me anymore?" he cooed

I stood listening to my brain crank out a list of possible responses. Tell the truth, lie, elude; the choices were plentiful. Finally, I selected one. A big step, tell the truth.

"I'm not in love with you."

"What?" he seemed genuinely surprised.

I walked away. He followed me.

"What do you mean?"

"You are not the same person I fell in love with. I...I don't know who you are."

He turned sobbing and ran back into the bedroom and threw himself on the bed. It was a typical teenage girl reaction. I didn't know what to do about that — so out of character for this fifty-year-old man, yet in character for who he was becoming.

This may have been a turning point, a turning away from each other. It did not change our outward appearance as a couple. It indicated a line drawn between us. In the wake of what was to come, I seem to have vacillated. After months of this torment between job and home, I had to choose. Was it a coin toss, a moment of whim? During our years together Martin had turned to me more than once asking permission to quit his job because he hated it. I knew he would get another one and always sided with him for his good. I decided it was time to get the same for myself. In doing so, I had to recommit to my marriage that I would continue to support him and to try and be open to what changes he had to go through. It was a tradeoff; I felt more of a commitment to him than to my employer.

I resigned my position. He came out to his current employer. He was released when they chose to close operations. We were both unemployed.

These were scary times. Neither of us had ever been in the situation before. Always had another job lined up before we quit. And always had the other if there was a break in our employment. But now... We took a home equity loan to cover our expenses. This wouldn't last forever, and we had a lot of equity in our home.

If we had known where our path led, would we have made the same choices?

A Year in Between

We begin the new year both unemployed. He was focused on living female as Maureen, so we took a line of credit on our home and dipped into savings.

I took back the reins to my gift basket business. Nine years before I bought this corporate gift basket business and enjoyed the creativity it required. The marketing and production planning were a natural evolution from what I had been doing with computers. But a whole lot of fun. I loved attending the gift shows and fancy food shows where I could meet face to face with vendors. The business's volume was enough to get recognition from them and be asked for ideas on new products.

While I had been earning a salary working elsewhere, I had let it run taking the risk that business would return. It had not. I had been operating with two full time and two part-time people but in truth it could run on less. With the market downturn, I reduced staff and ran it as tight as possible. At the peak, we were grossing half a million a year, with an average price of $50 a basket that means we were selling a lot of gift baskets. Business from the previous year was off by ten percent. Now I had the time and felt the duty to work out of the hole. It wasn't that we were losing customers, it was that the entire technology market cut back at the turn of the millennium.

Every day I went to the shop, the boys went to school, and Martin slept in, then rode his stationary bicycle. As most everyone knew about his choice to become a woman and his plans to have surgery, I no longer had to straddle the two realities. It didn't make it any easier for me to accept. I was still hoping that he would wake up and change his mind. He was awkward as Maureen and was not actively seeking employment because of it.

I suggested a 4th of July party, Martin invited members of his transgender group and old friends, I called friends and his cousin. The boys liked the idea. They were nervous, but I felt that if they saw others like their father, they might get some answers to their unasked question. Despite many one-on-one discussions, none of them were open to seeing a counselor. I didn't want to force it, but maybe this could bridge the gap in understanding. None of them exhibited behavior that indicated they were having problems; it was just awkward. After all they were in their teens, and that alone was awkward enough.

I don't know that I thought beyond that, inviting, planning a barbecue and watching fireworks. It seems unlike me, but I wasn't me then either. I wanted to put both groups of our friends together, I wanted to know what the life ahead might be like, which friends would I lose, which would stay with us.

Our home had a commanding view of the valley; we could sit on our deck and watch as many as six separate fireworks displays from Paramount's Great America in the north to Mirassou Winery to the south. It was a great setting for a party. People started arriving before dusk and food was laid out, everyone was introduced. Martin dressed as Maureen, slacks with a collared shirt, wig and makeup. Some of the TG group came as female, others as male. Martin's aunt and cousin came and were accepting; some of my closest friends were no shows. Later they would tell me that they just couldn't come, they couldn't accept what he was doing to his family and me. None of my sisters came, but I wasn't expecting them for this event. Everyone who came seemed to have an enjoyable time, and later the boys would share that some of the TGs were nice.

The boys played with fireworks and trouped in and out of the adults on the deck. They hung back and were assessing. They interacted with their father's cousin who was present and were happy to see him again. Martin's aunt was there, and she surprised me. While she hadn't been open to his news of wanting to be a woman, she had candid conversations with everyone there and later took me aside.

"Well, they all seem so normal. I'm glad I came," she said.

Everyone oohed and aahed over the displays and Martin and the boys set off quite a few of their own at the back of the yard. Around ten, everyone started saying their goodbyes and the evening ended. I felt a sort of comfort that there were no emotional meltdowns, and everyone seemed to get along well. Maybe things would work themselves out I hoped.

* * *

I was still in communication with my online support group with transgendered partners. The lead for this group was a trans person whose wife supported their family. Occasionally she would chime in, but for the most part, it was her Debbie who did the talking. It was a safe place to share our concerns and fears, ask questions of one another and try to cope. One day I received an email from Debbie. She said that a producer for the ABC television program 20/20 had contacted her and wanted to do a program on transgendered and their spouses who stood by them. She admitted that she had allowed this producer to view posts over the past few weeks. The producer had selected several of the group that she thought would be strong voices for the program. I was one of them.

I was taken aback first that the trust that we were safe from outsider's view had been broken. Then, I was delighted that the producer had singled me out. I weighed my response to the next question.

"Would it be alright for me to forward your email address to her?"

Saying yes might lead to being on national television — in prime time — sharing my story. Who mattered to me who didn't already know? What did I have to lose? What did I have to gain? What weighed heaviest was the fact that I could be an example, speak for others who might be finding themselves in the same or similar situation.

"Yes," I typed.

The producer contacted me later that day, she was quite complimentary about conversations I had while she was "listening in."

"I felt that you were a strong, confident voice and helpful to others," she said. Then she added, "Of course your husband will also need to appear on the show. We are hoping to have four couples for the taping."

"When?" I asked.

"Late December," she said.

That evening, I sat down with Martin and explained the situation. He furrowed his now plucked eyebrows and shook his head.

"I can tell this is something you would want to do, but it's not for me." Then as an afterthought, he asked, "Where would this be?"

"New York," I said.

He lit up. "We get a free trip to New York?"

I nodded.

"Okay, then," he said.

I don't know what he thought was going to be so magical about that, but that was the answer I wanted.

"When?" he asked.

"Late December she said."

"Oh, that won't work. I go in for facial reconstruction surgery the first week of December, and my face won't be healed for six weeks. Can they move it?"

"I'll ask," I said.

I wondered what I should wear to be interviewed on television. I wondered what Martin was dreaming about wearing. I was still stumbling over the facial reconstruction surgery. He had flown to Portland and met with the surgeon, and they had worked out a plan, but he didn't bring home any photos or blueprints for the reconstruction. I asked about the scope.

"It's really not that much," he began. "He'll trim my brow line, so it is not so pronounced and then pull my hairline forward so that it won't look as receding. He'll smooth out my jaw, so it isn't so squarely masculine. And while he is at it, he'll remove the bags from under my eyes."

I tried to imagine what his face would look like when all that was done.

"It'll be like a mini-facelift," he said cheerfully.

He said that to allay my concerns, but I could tell that like the teenage girl who covets a new outfit, this was not going to cure all ills.

"And then after the surgery, I'll go to Germany and have my vocal cords adjusted."

Pictures of Frankenstein swirled in my vision. We'll take this body, add that brain, sew it up here, cut it off there. I must have shown my distaste because he felt compelled to reassure me.

"This doctor is the best. He is highly recommended, and he just tightens up the cords to raise the voice a bit. It'll still sound like me, but my voice will be more like that of a woman."

Sound like a woman, I thought, you don't sound like a woman now. You sound like a spoiled little brat who is pretending to be someone they aren't. And will never be. It felt good to complete the thought, even if I didn't utter it aloud.

I called the producer and informed her of Martin's schedule. She said she didn't think moving it to the end of January would be a problem. She still didn't have four couples.

At the end of the first week of December, Martin flew to Portland for a day of preoperative tests. I came the night before surgery. December is my busiest time of year in the corporate gift basket business, and I needed to get in and get back as quickly as possible. I would be there when he came out of surgery. He would have to stay for the balance of the week before flying home.

I arrived late, after ten, and walked around the downtown area to tire myself out. My nerves felt frayed. I didn't know what to expect the next day. I didn't know how my husband would look and then I had to go and explain all this to the kids. What in the world was I doing? How had it gone this far?

Once this surgery started, there was no going back. The beard still grew in, of course not as thick as it used to, but despite electrolysis and laser removal, he still had to shave. But these surgical changes were going to be irreversible and noticeable, one step closer to being Maureen and not Martin.

I had no prior experience with plastic surgery. I did not know what to expect. I thought about pictures I had seen in magazines with headlines that blared "New Nose" or "Facelift," but those before and after photos, were not immediately after surgery.

The surgery took longer than anticipated — nearly five hours. They telephoned to let me know he was resting and that I should be able to come to see later that day.

After recovery, they wheeled him into his room,. He was groggy and had the foulest breath. I couldn't comment beyond that because his face was masked in gauze, his eyes peered out, but they were swollen nearly shut; his nose was taped over, and his jaw was bandaged, leaving only an opening for his lips.

Like so much else, I had not been privy to his conversation with the surgeon. Facial feminization was a long list of options depending on the male face to be changed and the desired results. I wondered if he had some work done on his nose as well. I couldn't picture him with a little turned up nose, not that his nose was too large or misshapen. If he had it changed, he would couch it in terms of correcting his snoring problem. His snores rumbled through the house, even with doors shut. The kids would laugh about how they heard dad snoring all the way in their bedrooms with the doors closed.

The doctor and nurses assured me that though the surgery had taken a little longer than expected, everything went well. He should expect a full recovery within six weeks; swelling should be down in two weeks and bruising would diminish with healing. There were no post-operative care instructions other than rest. The sutures would all dissolve and no follow up was needed. There wasn't much for me to do; smile, hold his hand.

As I flew home, I thought about the monster their father would look like for Christmas. There would be no putting a Santa suit on him this year.

The following week I picked him up at the airport. Again, without experience, I didn't know what to expect, but when I saw him sitting in a wheelchair, bandages still encircling his head and face, my heart plummeted.

"What?" I asked, not sure what I should say.

"No worries, this is normal. You should have seen the people on the plane staring at me. I let them think I was in an automobile accident."

We were four months before the sexual reassignment surgery which I nicknamed the 'whack it off." He didn't like it, but I held onto it as if it kept my sanity in balance. I knew the politically correct term, but not being in favor of it, I kept using my term. Regardless, it was looming close, and during the previous eight months Martin should have been living as a woman, and for the next four months, he should be living as a woman. He was still himself. When he went to his counseling or group sessions, he dressed as Maureen, but otherwise, he was Martin. I wondered over and over if this should be brought to the attention of his counselor, I questioned if this arrogance would betray him. I commented from time to time to him. I asked about clothing and dressing and hair, but he brushed aside my concerns. "I will when I am a woman," was his oft repeated response.

Which only made me wonder if he would stop this if he could see that he would not be a beautiful woman. Had his expectations been downgraded?

I was in a constant state of wondering what was going on — what was he thinking — could this all go away. I put one foot forward in front of the other.

It was pointed out to me that several times I mentioned here the sports bra and the painted toenails. Someone suggested I cut those references. My reaction was visceral. I had to live with that knowledge day in day out for several years, held to a secret pact. That repetition barely makes up for the number of times I had to blot it out of my mind to maintain my sanity. Somehow, I made it through.

Unraveling

In mid-January, I sat in an uncomfortable seat waiting for my flight to be called. I wore my favorite sweater and a thread caught by the buckle on my purse had been pulled. I stretched the sweater, trying to pull the thread back into place, but to no avail. I bit off the end freeing the trailing bit of yarn and pulled it quickly to snap it off. Then there was another loose yarn in its place, and I tugged it, thinking that if it came free, it might leave a wider row, but to my shock and alarm, it unraveled the hem of the sweater. I convinced myself that the hem was no big deal, and the sweater felt lighter and draped softer without that hem anyway, but there was no end to the fray, and suddenly I held a fistful of yarn.

143

They called my flight, and I bit off the end and tossed the yarn into the bin as I boarded the plane. On the plane, I took a window seat and kicked my bag under the seat in front of me. I closed my eyes and began the sorting out of feelings about where I was headed.

Like the sweater, my life was unraveling before my eyes, and I was unable to stop it. I went to the regional gift show in Los Angeles hoping to jump start the new year and my business. I sought some new product or idea to latch onto and get my energy rolling. I pushed myself to perform through the past holiday season, and I was not finding the motivation to move forward.

On the plane I thought about my marriage, it is always lurking there, waiting to be examined. I was married to a man who wanted to be a woman. Wanted? I had to face it – I was married to a man who was taking steps and would soon have surgery to become a woman. He had facial reconstruction surgery, and the bruises had all but gone away, I would soon be the wife to another woman who wanted me to love her as a woman. I felt backed into a corner. Why have I stayed? Because of the children, because of our life and the fact that apart, everything will have to change. Will it? I asked myself again. Will it have to change? Is there some way I can still go on?

144

Of course, I can and of course, the boys will find their way and be fine. But I hold back and do not want to call it quits. There's more here – delve deeper.

A year and a half before I had risen from bed, showered and then on my way to dress, he had lured me back to bed, and I said no. It was evident to me at that moment that I was repulsed by this person who I had so dearly loved. The gender thing was part of it; the fact that he lied to me and did not seem to tell me the whole truth even then, was at the foundation of this shift. He asked me then "don't you love me?" And I said that "I am no longer in love with you." I didn't say it mean, but I could not say yes – I could not lie. There were too many lies hidden like a mine field. I hoped he would understand the difference when I was not even sure. I hoped that this was a trough in our marriage, and I would rise out of it, and we would go on again.

Maybe that was the day from which everything changed. I can only think about it now and wonder, but maybe it was the day he spat out "I want to be a woman" in marriage counseling. All those things knitted together and made a chasm that could not be filled or leapt.

The marriage counselor asked me about our sex life. I turned to Martin who had told me that our sex life and his gender issues were not to be discussed.

The jump to this after so many sessions where it has not been addressed threw me off guard. We were paying for this counseling so why were we not taking advantage of help?

Head down, looking at my hands in my lap; I said, "Martin prefers masturbation." There was silence. I imagined Martin puffing up, ready to strike with some hurtful words, but when I looked, it was the Queen of Hearts sitting on her throne, and Martin and I sat as co-defendants in her court.

"So, you don't enjoy sexual intercourse?" she snarled at Martin.

"It's not that," he said.

"Well, then you are not able to perform?"

"It's not that," he said.

"Well ..."

"It's that I want to be a woman," he said.

I was shaken to my core as this is what I had long feared, but he had never verbalized it.

"And how do you feel about this Alice?" she demanded.

I had no snappy comeback, no well thought out response, so when in doubt, I spat out the truth. "I don't want to be married to a woman."

There was a quiet moment, the three of us caught, digesting those words.

Martin jumped up from his chair, "I'm done." He stormed out of the room.

146

The Queen of Hearts was gone, and the marriage counselor was back, sitting on the other side of the table. She said, "I think that we should still continue."

Over time, I began to wonder if I missed something. Did Martin and this marriage counselor have a session together without me? Did they confer on this subject? Was this the reason why he suddenly acquiesced to counseling to get this out on the table in public? I felt the presence of the Cheshire Cat.

"So, you are starting to catch on?" he smirked.

When I replay that scene, the marriage counselor was the Queen of Hearts, and she laughed at me, laughed at me for so naively thinking that Martin was there to find the truth. Or was she laughing at me because I thought I could still stop Martin from this gender bender course?

I spent most of my middle adult years (from 26 to 41) working in the electronics industry. There connectors were labeled as male or female, and when the connections didn't line up, often they would have to add an adaptor which would change a male connection to female (or the other way around), and this handy little device was called a gender bender. Is this where Martin got the idea that changing from male to female wasn't so difficult?

The pilot announced that we were approaching our destination and landing shortly. I sunk deeper into my thoughts still hoping to find the way out of this rabbit hole.

Over the past ten years of our marriage, we performed this little dance. It started that many years ago on Christmas Eve in the closet when he told me he wanted to dress in women's clothes. Then I cried, and we didn't talk about it for several years. As he suffered through the diagnosis of lymphoma and chemo, he turned over in his mind the question of what he wanted to do before he died and again, he told me that he wanted to see if he could be a woman. I resisted helping him, he sought others and then yearned to be part of the counseling group. It was when he confessed to me that he was buying hormones on the Internet. I agreed to be supportive and urged him to do it "by the book." Little by little, step by step he lured me through the maze to this point. Wanting to or not, I came this distance and am as disgusted by the final step as he is excited by it. In just three months he will be legally and physically a woman. Who will I be?

There had been hints from Martin, threats that my acceptance of his gender change was not all the changes he would require.

Scene 1: Martin asked me if I wanted to take dance lessons. I always loved to dance, but Martin felt uncomfortable, and there were only a few times that he ventured out onto a dance floor with me. "Of course," I said thrilled that now he would be willing to learn, and I fast forward to how much fun it will be to have a dance partner. But the Queen of Hearts prodded me with the next question "Who will lead?" and Martin said to me, "Well I thought I could be the girl and this time you could be the man." The Queen snickered and tsked at her Jacks to move along.

Scene 2: I found Martin one night sitting in bed with a magazine and looking at pictures of wedding dresses. "We could have another wedding," he said to me. I looked over his shoulder at the page of elegant wedding gowns and asked, "What would you wear?"

He said, "I always wanted to be a bride."

The Queen of Hearts was breathing down my neck, exhaling through her nostrils like a bull about to charge. Her hot breath raised the hair on the nape of my neck.

"And you could wear the tux this time," he said nonchalantly turning the page.

It was not about me helping, letting, or supporting him through his gender transition, it was also about me stepping from my role and changing to better serve him. How far would I go?

The descent started. The attendant stood in the aisle with the open trash bag. I reached for my empty cup and realized that I had another handful of yarn. I pressed the yarn into the cup and tossed it into her bag. I hoped that I could uncloud my mind, but the result is that we are done, not that there is a cure or a fix. I've stretched myself as far as I could and have almost lost me.

In our twenty years together, Martin never met me at an airport. He always provided curbside pick-up. I unloaded with the passengers and started the trek through the airport, but there he was at the gate to greet me. Seeing him, I was surprised. Our meeting was awkward, like estranged friends, not like lovers. We walked to the car in the parking lot, sat down, and seat belted up. He turned on the engine and paid at the booth. As he maneuvered through the roundabout exit, he turned to me.

"We will sell the house, divorce and split everything."

Why now? I questioned, but instead of asking, I sat and let the tears fall. He was also crying. I knew this is what must happen, but just as I was a passenger in the car, I felt I had been a passenger through all the twists and turns of our relationship.

Later, there was a moment. We were arguing. He was telling me we had to divorce because soon he would be a woman and he wanted to be loved as one.

My next statement formed in my brain. How dare he use that on me when I am a woman, and he is trying to make me over to what he wants – not loving me as I am. Words form faster in your brain than flow out your mouth and as they began to form on my tongue there was an audible click. I turned away from him in reaction to the sound. It was the Cheshire Cat sucking his teeth.

How often had I thought of the difficulty in negotiating a civil divorce from this man. Now he was bartering for that. Why did I want to stand in his way? I discarded the thought, closed my mouth and accepted.

In doing so, we split everything evenly and he provided for the boy's needs and schooling.

Over the next couple of days, we sorted out what and when before we tell the children. It was January, Martin's surgery was scheduled for April. He expected me to accompany him on that trip. One night as I passed through the bedroom, I heard the click click of him typing on the keyboard.

As usual, he slapped the laptop shut.

"What are you doing?"

"Nothing."

"Who are you communicating with?" I let fly the accusation. "Is this the person you think you are in love with?"

He hung his head, "Yes."

"Then fine, she can go be nursemaid to you." I stormed out of the room. I was confused. How much more did I owe Martin? There was hurt over my efforts to support him, and his lack of concern for me and the boys with all these changes. And now he told me that he is in love with this woman he has only met online. The only thing I knew about her is what he told me. "She says I am the most feminine girl she has met."

I called the 20/20 producer and told her we would be unable to participate; we were no longer going to be together. She said she was sorry to hear that and wished me well. I kept an eye out for the program.

After much thought, I let my online group know that we had decided to divorce and signed off. I could see no reason to continue, and I did not want to be a negative voice. I missed the daily interaction, but I had a lot of decisions to make.

Even after leaving the group, I wondered how each of them met their future and which ones would be able to stay with their partner and which ones would not. I prayed that they would be able to accept whichever fate they met. By the time the program finally aired, I had to fortify myself to sit down and watch it without interruption. None of the participants were ones I recognized by their names or stories.

I calmed down and got back in stride. I drew a decision tree: find a job or leave the area. I made a list of five locations that I found suitable to consider for relocation. I sent resumes and contacted people to let them know I was ready to get back into the workforce. The toughest decision had to do with the fact that selling the house left me with enough money to buy a fixer but no money to do the fixing. The boys would be leaving this magnificent home and moving into a house they would find objectionable. Relocation meant them leaving their friends and the only neighborhood they had ever known. My list of wants included getting out of the rat race and starting over in a small town, near the water, with neither too hot summers or too cold winters and real seasonal changes. If I left the area, I would have to sell the business as well.

After meeting with realtors and looking at comparable properties, I wrote out a long list of things that needed to be done before we put the house on the market. I wrote out a plan for the next three months; bring a dumpster on the property, get rid of everything that was broken, ugly or unused. Next was replacing the carpeting throughout the home and repainting my beautiful colorful walls to neutral.

Martin pranced around the house in his bike shorts and black sports bra, between the bedroom and the family room where he rode a stationary bicycle. He had thirty pounds to lose before surgery in April. His need was always greater than courtesy to any of us also in the house. I had a couple of people I was working on a contract job with, and in the middle of our meeting in the dining room, Martin trotted by. Of course, he wore the bra and bike shorts, but no wig, no makeup. "Who's that?" their looks said, but they didn't verbalize. I was left to ignore it or explain it.

The boys got used to seeing their father like that and didn't say anything about it, but they also didn't bring friends into the house anymore.

The bruises on Martin's face were finally gone. I had to look hard to see the difference. The brow ridge was less pronounced as was the jaw line, but he still looked like himself. He did not have an overtly feminine face to begin. The bags under his eyes were gone, making him look younger, less tired. The hairline though was a Frankensteinian stitch up. They had cut the skin at the hairline, then peeled it down to trim the ridge, then pulled it up and tucked it under the scalp. There was an angry red scar that ran across the top of his forehead, and rather than smooth there was a noticeable lump. He sat in front of the mirror and pushed and pulled and complained. Did he call the surgeon or go for a follow-up? Not that I ever knew. With still not enough hair growth in the area, he would need to cover it with a wig.

This was the year that Martin should have been living as a woman full-time. But unless he was going somewhere as Maureen, he wore his same clothing. I mentioned this to him on a couple of occasions.

"I thought you were supposed to be Maureen twenty-four seven."

"I am."

"But you are still dressing like Martin."

He shrugged. "So, it's easier. No one sees me anyway."

I listened and registered that I had been regulated to "no one."

I wondered where all these short cuts would take him.

Suddenly, I was untethered, feeling discarded. Pitying myself that I had come along all this way and now he turned to the internet to find love. On the other hand, I didn't need to keep trying to make myself over to fit his new future.

I paid attention to what I set as my priorities —— made sure that I negotiated for what was best for the boys and me.

Exit Strategy

I like to make New Year resolutions. Like everyone, I have a hard time sticking with them. Each year I devise one or two that I will follow through. I began that year thinking about it, then committed to walking one thousand miles. Not a journey to someplace, just a goal to calculate purposeful walking and a way to get myself into better shape. The first day I walked one mile, the next day two. After a week, I reviewed my progress and began to write the number of miles each day on a calendar. Then I did the math. To achieve my goal, I should be putting in an average of three miles a day for a total of two hundred fifty miles per quarter. That was a lot more than what I had been doing.

Having to deal with an impending divorce and all that entailed, fueled me to step outside the door and pound the pavement. I consulted a map and plotted three-mile hikes around the neighborhood. I dropped the boys at school and drove a couple of miles to a park and covered five miles in a little over an hour. It was serene nature at its best, and I sorted out my feelings and stretched my mind for what I needed.

Martin would see me preparing for a walk and ask to come along. Soon I learned that all he wanted was to talk about his plans for his life as a woman. It was all about clothing and how he would look. If I objected or questioned, he would remind me that we were BFFs (best girlfriends). We were not – or rather, I could not envision any way that we could be.

I told him that if he came along, there would be no girl talk. He'd agree but then quickly jump back into whatever was on his mind and prattle on about camis or how many months till he could schedule the surgery or types of surgeries he should have to feminize his facial features as well as the sexual reassignment surgery.

One day we were at the park, and I carried an umbrella as it was occasionally sprinkling. He started in again, and I lost it. I smacked that umbrella into the pavement as hard as I could time and time again. I think that was the last time I let him walk with me.

The walks were my means of burning off the anxiety and him coming along only accelerated it.

By the end of March, I had accumulated the two hundred and fifty miles completed to be on goal. But the month earlier I purchased a new pair of shoes, and they did not support my feet as they should have. All that pounding took its toll. I would finish my walk dragging my right foot.

The diagnosis was simple – plantar fasciitis on both feet. I could not keep up the walking, so I switched to water aerobics and enlisted my sister as my teammate. I joined her gym, and we would work out three mornings a week. I added two more night classes, and I was sleeping soundly despite the emotional stress in my life.

There were decisions to be made. If I could land a position with a six-figure income and benefits, I could stay in the house. If I couldn't find the job, then we'd have to sell. If I stayed in the area, I could afford little; housing prices had risen dramatically since we purchased our home and even though the market was not robust, my half would mean I had to buy a fixer, but I would not have money to do the fixing.

I sat one afternoon in the park with a piece of paper and drew a decision tree. Do`I stay or go? If I stay, I need to get a job. If I go, where do I go? I had been at this juncture before.

When I married my high school sweetheart, he was in the Navy, and we were stationed away. When his duty ended, we came back to where our families lived. After that marriage ended, I could have moved anywhere, but I clung to my family for support. Now, I had another opportunity to start over, try someplace new. The thought of that intrigued me.

I made a list of five areas where I might relocate. They were chosen based on several factors. First was economics; the locale was less expensive living than where I was. The second was location, not too hustle bustle but still had a nice climate. I wrote in the margin; I would like to live in a small town, near the water and in a place where I could be free to be myself. This last one came from having to dress for success and be a part of the corporate world. The five cities I listed were not yet researched, just some ideas. I would then spend time doing my research and investigating what was to come.

After six weeks of phone calls and interviews, there was no job on the horizon. I bit the bullet and called the real estate office. There were changes I needed to make to put the house on the market. I planned: one week to clean up outside, one week inside, one-week re-carpet upstairs one-week re-carpet downstairs, paint, etc.

There was another timeline running in parallel. In the first week of April, I flew to Wisconsin with Martin. We checked him into the hospital where he was scheduled for surgery, and I checked into an Extended Stay motel. That night I realized that the man I married would be no more. In the morning, I awoke to snow. I got a call just after noon that

Maureen was resting comfortably, and I could come for a visit. I drove cautiously to the hospital and went to her room. She lay in a hospital bed with the typical cotton gown. She smiled at me, happy to see me, then without a pause, she shared.

"See," she said. Her voice was filled with delight. She kicked back the sheet and lifted the gown.

I thought she wanted to show me her breasts, but with the raising of the gown, she was wanted to show me that she was indeed a she down there as well. I quickly glanced away.

There on the floor near the wall was a red and white six-pack cooler, like the one used to for soft drinks. I thought of the coolers they use to transport body parts for transplants. Were they keeping his penis on ice should he change his mind? As soon as I thought that I knew that couldn't be, they had already taken it apart and reused it. The cooler was for ice packs. Still, the image and idea were there for my entertainment.

Making an excuse about the weather and the forecast for more snow, I quickly fled the hospital and returned to the safety of my room. What I had tried to keep from happening, had happened. What was I going to do now?

The recovery was quick. The next day they had her up and walking. The hospital was no longer required, so she moved to a hotel where they kept their patients for the next week and a half. The patients were checked by nurses but were to start taking care of their new bodies and learning how to do so. Once the packing was removed from the new cavity in their bodies, they had to use a dildo to preserve the opening. This was indeed not a sex toy but a surgical stainless-steel shaft, in fact, they had to buy these in graduated sizes and work up from the smallest to the largest, holding it in place for ten minutes several times a day.

I had much to think over in my motel room, calls to the kids to check in and be sure they were doing well, assuring them that dad was doing well and confirming when I would be back. Each day I would go and make a short visit and take a short walk. I wasn't thinking beyond the day, the next day. I was easily overwhelmed with all the changes in play.

Maureen wanted to drive from Appleton, Wisconsin to Chicago and fly home after a visit with her brother and his family. She had made reservations at a hotel, and when we checked in, I found that she had a reserved a room with a single queen bed. There were no vacancies, and I could not make any changes.

I laid awake watching the dim light on the smoke detector as I recounted our years together. With terms of our divorce worked out, less than a month till she left the family home, my recollections were cruelly honest. I faulted myself for not asking questions, not laying down the law and letting things go by. Perhaps it was the lack of sleep or my less than happy thoughts, but the next day we would have the biggest of all our disagreements. Not only was it a screaming match, but we were seated beside each other speeding along an Interstate at seventy miles per hour.

The gist of the argument was Maureen's power struggle with her father. As he had not agreed to meet her as Maureen, she wanted me to keep the children from their grandparents. Her reasoning was that if he was not allowed access to the grandchildren, he would relent and accept her as his daughter. On the other hand, these were the only living grandparents the children had, and I was not about to put them on any bargaining table. The yelling reached a pitch then she screamed, "I thought I could count on your support." That sent me off on another round.

"You have had my support. This isn't about support; this is about taking something more away from the children." This was a release for me and an unfiltered honest response. It was like a declaration of independence.

The argument petered out as we reached the airport and returned the rental car. The flight home was in silence. At home, she slipped into bed.

I caught up with the kids, checked on what I needed to get done, groceries I needed to buy and slept in the office upstairs. The dogs followed me and slept with me. The boys knew about the impending divorce and that I slept in the office now. We never talked more about it.

The boys like to the tell the story about the day their mother stood on the deck outside the kitchen yelling. They don't remember what it was about. I do.

Maureen was in the master bedroom, with its own bathroom and everything she needed. She picked up the telephone next to the bed and called the house on the second phone line. I answered in the kitchen while tutoring homework and preparing dinner.

"Hi," I said.

"It's me," she said.

"What?"

"I need a tissue."

I looked at what I was doing and countered that with what she was doing, lying in bed thinking only of herself. I hung up the phone, stepped out the door onto the deck, and screamed.

I released the tension that had been building and the frustration. The hurt feelings I may have harbored were completely wiped away by this behavior. Had she always been this self-centered and unaware of everyone in the house?

There were tissues in the bathroom not six feet away from where she lay. She was not confined to bed. This was another attempt to have me favor her. I was done.

When I returned from Wisconsin, a dumpster had been placed in the driveway, and the boys and I walked around the house. If it was broken, unused or ugly, it went into the dumpster. When full, we called and ordered another. Maureen would walk around and comment, "You're not throwing that out?" or "What's wrong with that?" She had already laid claim to what she wanted and planned to take when she left the house. She was planning on moving out by the end of June.

The following week, the boys and I moved all the furnishings from the upstairs three bedrooms into the office. Then the carpet layers came and installed the new neutral carpet in the three bedrooms and on the stairway. The following week, we did the same with the living room furniture and the furniture in the master bedroom. Everything was moved into the hall or family room, and then the carpet layers did their job.

The for-sale sign went up on the front lawn. Everything was clean and neat inside and out. Now the waiting began.

One more detail to consider, if I left the area, I had to sell my business. This was not a good time to do so; we were still feeling the effects of the dot-bomb recession. I let it be known to a small circle of people who might have an interest. As the days passed, I negotiated with my landlord and worked out a deal to vacate my space at the end of the summer. It was kind of them to let me break my lease. I was sure that they would be able to bring in a new tenant or expand the one next door into the space.

In June, the boys finished school, and I suggested a scouting trip to an area I chose. They were unhappy about the choices their parents were making. It was time to try and persuade them to consider options. My older two sons Henry and Sam intended to stay where they were. Henry was already out on his own, and Sam had just completed his first year of college. Max and Arlo would be starting their sophomore year in high school. The worst age to transplant kids. We loaded up the car and made the nine-hundred-mile trek to Washington state. The good news was that we got to spend time with two of my sisters and their children as well as take a walk through several homes on the market. The area won me over; I felt positive and joyful while the boys were disgusted and negative.

When we returned home, we found that their father, Maureen had left. She had agreed to stay there with Sam until we returned, but she didn't. I felt relieved to have her gone, but her untimely departure left a feeling of abandonment in my youngest sons.

"I didn't even say goodbye," Max said.

"He didn't say goodbye," Arlo said.

They stormed off to their rooms.

The boys were left with a feeling of abandonment. Their father's involvement in their lives never met their expectations or wanting.

While I offered counseling, they chose to deal with their feelings alone — perhaps with each other. For several years long car rides allowed us to talk out our feelings.

Moving On

In August, I laid off my two remaining employees. I had announced to them in July that I would be selling the business and moving out of the facility. They were both able to secure other jobs in the interim. My son, Henry had been employed with me for almost the entire nine years I owned the business. He helped me move from the space into a rented storage facility. We set up shelving and stored our inventory. I had been reducing inventory over the summer, selling off unique and odd pieces at the local flea market. As much as it seemed monumental, it all worked out smoothly.

I remember sweeping out the space when it was empty, reviewing the highlights of the nine years and feeling the presence of the two women who had started the business before me. It was a healing closure.

But I hadn't closed the business. I continued to take phone calls and online orders. I'd make a run to the storage facility, pick up what I needed, head home, make up the gift baskets and deliver them. I kept the downsizing from my clients, and it was enough to keep paying the bills.

In October, everything came together. I got an offer on the house and an offer on the business. In fact, one day, I accomplished three things. I countered the offer on the house, I wrote up the purchase and sale agreement on the business, and I wrote out the terms of our divorce agreement. Like other things Maureen agreed to do this but never got around to it. The next day I received agreement on all three.

I didn't get all the terms I wanted, but I got what I needed. The buyers of the house agreed to close by the end of October and allow me to stay in the home until the middle of December, enough time for the boys to finish the school term. I made a quick trip back to Washington to look at houses and made an offer on one. By Monday, I had acceptance and was busy moving the inventory to the business buyer's location and training them.

Having no first-hand experience with making a long-distance move, I sought advice and ended up renting space on a commercial moving van with the agreement that I do the loading and unloading. I had no idea what that entailed. I will forever be thankful for family members because, without them, it would never have been accomplished. I suggest that you don't do what I did.

One sister said her husband might be available to come over and then I had Henry and Sam to help. I knew how to pack, and the boys and I had everything ready to go onto the truck, but no idea how to load it. My brother-in-law took charge. and it all fit. The truck driver even took a couple of things in his cab to help. The truck pulled out of the driveway, and two of my sisters were busy cleaning. At ten that night, the new owners showed up, and I walked them through and left.

Max and Arlo had opted to go with friends after school that day, and they never came back to see the house empty. I drove Sam to his new apartment and dropped him there. I picked up Max and Arlo, the dogs, and we checked into a motel for the night. The next morning, we headed north.

In two days, we arrived at my sister's home. We celebrated Christmas and the boys' fifteenth birthdays amid family. It was a welcomed respite. The day before Christmas, we drove the two hours to our new home to meet the moving truck and unload it. While I had the same number of people to unload it as there had been to load it, I was the only common denominator. When the mattresses were being pulled off, I tried to recall what someone had said when they loaded them. I remembered in time. "Watch out, there's a glass tabletop in there," I shouted as it came flying out. We caught it and other than one picture frame which cracked, there was no damage. The big screen TV, the grandfather clock, and all the stuff made the move. We left everything in the house and returned to my sister's home to celebrate the holiday.

On the twenty-seventh, we reloaded our car and made the journey to our new home. As the car crested a hill on a remote highway, I watched the precipitation change from rain to snow. I had been making a mental list of what I needed to do. Buy new hook ups for the washer and dryer, go to the grocery store, pick up something for dinner. Now I was worried about being caught in a snowstorm and being without food.

"Is that snow?" Arlo asked.

Both boys had been asleep. I alone had witnessed the white stuff.

"Looks like it," I said.

"What?" Max said from the back seat.

"Snow," Arlo said.

"Where?" Max said.

By then it was back to rain and half a mile further, it was dry.

At the house, Max and Arlo began to sort out their belongings and set up their beds. I let the dogs into the backyard and watched to see that they could not escape the fencing. Then I headed to town to fulfill that shopping list.

Over the next few weeks, we settled into our new home. The boys sulked and acted disinterested.

I found myself having to deal with hurt feelings, fear, and guilt. I had been stuck trying to help my partner and willing to let go of myself – then finding that I had lost touch with me. I remember the day I asked myself what color I wanted to paint the walls in my bedroom, and I did not know. That was terrifying to me as I had always known before what pleased me, making the decision was not the difficult part, it was the fact that looking inward I found emptiness.

I purchased a stack of magazines and started flipping pages, ripping out those that had something I liked, or was curious about. Then I started pasting them into a scrapbook, thinking all the while that I was finding my likes. The scrapbook was barely half full when I started incorporating those things into my life. I was thankful that I chose to take a new path, go on an adventure, recreate my life in a whole new place with all new people because through that I found myself, made myself better than I was, and avoided becoming the victim of my circumstances.

I am not a victim; I am a survivor.

That began the next chapter in my life. I enjoyed the rediscovery as I embarked on a course that built on my skills and experience leading me to venture into creativity.

Understanding

Five years later, I needed to drive back to California to pick up Max and bring him home. He had moved back to live with his brother, and it was time for him to come home. Maureen heard that I was going to be driving and called to ask if she could ride along. She was ready with the fact that she could share in the driving and help pay for gas. I agreed because I needed to drop off some things I no longer wanted that she wanted. Even as I drove the four hours to her home, I wondered what I would do with her in the car for the next twelve-hour drive.

Before we were beyond her city limits, she turned to me.

"I think my life was better with you. There should be some way we could get back together."

We had been down this road many times already, and I didn't want to come out and say what I was thinking. Are you kidding? Instead, I turned the conversation to how she might improve her life.

"Are you getting out? Doing things?"

The answer was the same the last dozen times. It wasn't her fault that her partner didn't want to, and her partner didn't want her doing things without her. So, one excuse led to another. There was nothing I could offer that she would consider. She repeatedly brought the conversation back around to reuniting.

I stopped trying to converse with her and watched the traffic. Something was on the periphery coming into focus, and I needed to allow it to materialize. Once again in my life was the feeling that what was going on was not about me.

I flashed back to when she was coming out to relatives and friends. In telling me she would repeat their question to her. "What does Alice have to say about this?" She would shrug this off. "I don't know why they ask that, this is not about you, it's about me."

Her thought that this had nothing to do with me irritated me. It had everything to do with me. This was not a change just for her. It impacted all of us. How could she not see that this was more than about her, it affected me Was she so blind to us?

Now she wanted to have conversations about us getting back together. Now it's her turn to want what she cannot have. First, I am heterosexual and second, is she not aware that she burned all the bridges with me? Does she not realize that she made her decision and left the home, left it all in my hands to handle? What is she thinking suggesting that we get back together?

"This has nothing to do with me, does it?" I asked the Cheshire cat, the one who traveled in my head and helped me sort out things.

"What do you mean?" he slyly asked.

"She's not suggesting that we get back together for my benefit."

"It might be entertaining to ask her how you would benefit."

I almost laughed out loud. The spell was broken. I had been so caught up in how to please him/her, help him/her, support him/her, that I stopped thinking of how this benefited me. Even as she tried to persuade me to consider, it was one-sided. Though she supported herself for all these years on savings, I had worked safeguarding my savings.

"Give me one way that it will benefit me," I wanted to say, but it felt too cruel to utter. She was grasping.

Maureen didn't need to answer; there was no way. She had plowed through most of her savings and had been unable to get hired back into her field. She didn't have the confidence to be the woman that she now was. She faulted her voice for being too low but was unwilling to accept that some women have lower voices. Some women are misunderstood on the telephone to be male, and I explained how I had a friend who no matter what he said sounded like a woman on the phone.

Instead of dismissing the error and moving on, she adopted a breathy whisper that was supposed to sound feminine. Too often people told me they gave up conversing with her because they could never hear what she was saying. I had experienced the same thing. Here in the car, she spoke in her normal voice, sounding like the old Martin.

After several hours, I said I could use a break and asked if she would drive.

"Not now, I'm sleepy."

I popped the top on another can of caffeine.

When we arrived, I dropped her off as planned and said goodbye. I went on to my son's place, and as I settled in for the night, I realized that she did not help with the driving or pay for gas. I got suckered again. But there was a calm relief within me. It was in my past, in perspective, I finally understood.

A deeper understanding followed. One that involved the setup for my failure to recognize the potential for hurt. We grow up believing that what we know is what the world is all about. My parents had a love story – one that seemed to last through their lifetime. Looking back through adult eyes I can see that they had some struggles and a lot of difficulties to overcome, but they were there for each other. I expected that to be the case for myself and whoever would be my partner. I could not even fathom that it could be another way. It took two failed marriages, two broken hearts to get me to take a deeper look and to realize that not everyone will follow the example of my parents – no matter how hard I tried.

My journey was complete. I read somewhere that sometimes a part of us must die before another part can come to life. I needed to let go of my need to help and accept. I needed to learn to really see and hear where I fit and not to accept less than what I deserved.

Following my start over, I had a wonderful new career in real estate and made many new friends. I am somewhat surprised by how many trans people and trans family members I meet. Maybe it is because of my own involvement but I welcome them and do not judge.

Postscript – 2015

Twelve years after Martin and I separated and started our lives over, Bruce Jenner came out as trans. This prompted my son, Max to comment on Facebook. The following are excerpts of his postings and comments from Maureen, and Sam. I add this to provide insight on the boys understanding.

From Max:

These two posts are for sure insights into my own life but not for sympathy. I saw Bruce's interview on TV and saw similarities to my life. I doubt he or his kids will see this, but it needed saying. I wanted to give insight into those affected by his decision.

Initial post:

I'm watching the documentary on Bruce Jenner. It makes me think of my father, Martin and his transition to Maureen. A man who in secrecy either from shame or fear, hid his intentions from his family. Secret toenail paintings and nightgown partaking in private with my mother. I was 13 if I remember right.

I walked in to say goodnight and kiss my parents on the cheek as I often did.

We all had our things with him. Henry, if I recall, was a rebel, Dad and Sam got along with tech and Trek, Arlo finances, and I with little to choose from, chose stature and weightlifting.

I wanted to emulate my father, 6 feet tall, 300 lbs and limbs like tree trunks. He was a man's man — tools, exercise, chest hair, and grunting — that typical masculine stuff. Needless to say, he was my guiding light to manhood, and in an instant the light went out, the stars faded, and I was a puberty-stricken boy lost at sea.

Metaphors aside, I walked in that night to kiss my parents before I went off to sleep. When I walked in, there across the room in the bathroom stood a large pink robe. Mom? A tall lady? Dad! I apologized in shock backed away and made it halfway up the stairs when the tears began to fall. I crawled up the rest of the flight and into bed crying. "Oh my god my dad's gay, he's gay..." I didn't know what I had seen, what I witnessed. A game? A farce? I'm missing something...

He came in his slacks and work shirt, the same dirty dusty clothes he always wore. There was no make-up, no toenail polish, at least that I could see. He wore his socks. He told me "Your mom and I were just kidding, it's nothing."

He asked me to give him a back scratch, something I'd done often for my dad. I scratched in wavy patterns down his back similar to a game kids played to give each other chills. About halfway down, I could feel something catch my nails. It was obscure so I continued. I realized he was wearing a bra. He left repeating, "It's fine. There's nothing to worry about. I'm not gay." And that was it.

Shortly after that, he came out to my family. He had us all at the dinner table, my brothers, mom and me. The details are vague. I just remember he told us, and Arlo shut down that day. I remember how quiet he got. Just nothing to say. No expression. It's always felt to me like he never came back. Different somehow like he needed more info or something.

Sam and I battled over who knew first. You see he was still Martin. Just Martin who says he wants to be a woman. Martin who says he's still our dad. Of course, as children we believed it. We supported him, we wanted everything to stay the same. He changed his appearance, and then he left.

Everything changed and in the end nothing got better. Nothing changed in him.

So Bruce, I ask you to think about what you are doing and that if it's truly what you want because support may fade, love may too, and when you are left in your new body, will they accept you? I hope so.

I apologize if my opinion offends anyone.

Maureen's response to Max:

I never knew much of what you have written. I did the best I could at the time. It is a very difficult and frightening thing. And there's always 20-20 hindsight. Maybe after a dozen years you'd like to talk about it?

Max's response to Maureen:

We talked about it at your home. Honest, I'm good. What's done is done. I just felt compelled to speak about something I didn't do when you made this decision all those years ago. I never said or thought about long-term getting your approval and you being happy.

And with how it turned out, I wish I had said what I wanted. I wish I'd thought about it. I couldn't and that's fine but maybe there is some small chance they will if they read it and it helps, but for me this was closure.

I had an opportunity to say what I didn't. It's really not that big of a deal. I'm sorry if I offended you or made you worry.

Max's 2nd post

Thinking about last night's emotionally-fueled post, I wanted to say "sorry dad" for putting you in the blast. When I heard what Bruce was saying, I saw a still struggling man. Despite the changes, despite his façade, he looked to be in pain and out of sorts. This false bravado fueled by a similarity in situation and circumstances compelled me to post something on the subject. I know that some would say his situation is not your own, but it wasn't just for Bruce that I posted that, it was for his kids. I wanted to express a traumatic change, a family's want to stay the same, and how that affects not only ourselves but my father. To this day I feel partially responsible for a false hope I may have established with you. I wanted my father's affection, respect, and to be him. I finally had something more than a back scratch. In the process I gave him acceptance, but it wasn't for the right reasons and in my mind I feel like if I could have just been honest and maybe you wouldn't have gone through with it. I realize it's a choice and more personal than anything, but there are always other factors.

Sam's response to Max:

Glad to see your finally becoming more open about it. You and Arlo had the brunt of it since you were still young when it happened.

The truth of it was, for me at least, more about who he was when he was our age, what Dad revealed to us wasn't what he wanted to be or what he felt was necessarily the proper man, but what Grandpa had made him believe was the only way to be a man.

I don't think he knew how much we would pick up on his macho man attitude he always put on.

None of us can say we agree with the way he did it, but I am glad he did it. If it is who he truly wanted to be, regardless of the major obstacles he will have to overcome. He should be who he really wants to be, he worked hard and raised four boys, battled cancer and won. He dealt with having a seriously judgmental family, and somehow raised us without it.

It's easy since we were his kids to see all that crazy and all that bad, but as adults we can start to look back and see all the good, we had that so many didn't.

I'm glad to see you're opening up about it, because this means you are now one step closer to understanding what it must have taken for him to make the choices he did, and what it means to him to one day have his sons back in his life.

Epilog

Holidays

In the year we divorced, Maureen returned in November and we celebrated the holidays as a family. She stayed for a week, and she slept on the floor in the living room, allowing me the master bedroom.

In subsequent years, we would facilitate this family gathering at Christmas. Often, she came to our home, once we went to hers, a couple of times we gathered at the home which two of our sons shared in California. I facilitated these get togethers because I wanted the boys to have some relationship with their father, some closure.

Both of my husbands, Martin and the one before, had suffered their parents' divorces as teens, and both told me of the isolation they felt. I worked hard to alleviate that for my sons. Although they continued to refuse any outside counseling, long car trips often turned into conversations about their feelings, asking and answering questions.

At one holiday gathering, even though three of the four boys were present, Maureen seemed to spend her time following me around and talking with me. Realizing this, I knew that I needed to exit the picture so that the true meaning of these get togethers, interaction for the boys with their father would happen.

A Graduation

Arlo was the first to earn his bachelor's degree. From early in his life, his father told him how important it was to get a college education. Throughout his school years, he heard his father say that he would support them if they were in college. He was the youngest and the first to achieve this goal. There was a stumbling block before the ceremony. He had to tell the parents of his girlfriend about his father now being a woman. Though they had dated for four years, there had never been a mention of this or a question from them. He asked me for advice. Finally, he sat down with her father and explained that his father was now a woman.

"That is something. I'm not surprised because I knew there was something you weren't saying."

"What do you think your wife will say? Will you be okay meeting her?"

"Don't worry. I'll explain it. We will be fine."

I didn't talk with Maureen but was saddened when she did not appear for the ceremony. Claiming some last-minute emergency, she did not make the

four-hour drive to watch her son accept his diploma.
I sat in the stands and cheered him.

A Wedding

Four years later, Arlo and his fiancé married.
Invitations were carefully worded to read "the parents
of" Arlo and Linda" invite you to the wedding.
Maureen arrived dressed as Martin. She trudged
across the lawn to sit next to me at the rehearsal.

"I forgot how expensive men's clothing can be,"
she said.

"Why didn't you come as Maureen?" I asked
knowing that Arlo had worked hard to explain his
father's appearance as a woman which didn't
materialize.

She shrugged, "I just thought it would be better
this way. I bought two suits and got a new hairpiece."

I looked at her. She was dressed in a dark blue
pin striped suit, white shirt, navy blue tie. On her feet
were men's dress shoes and, on her head, a new Hair
Club for Men hairpiece. She had little or no beard,
trimly plucked eyebrows. Her appearance was odd,
something not quite male, nor female.

I nodded and looked away.

"I had to wear two bras to hold in my breasts,"
she said.

I felt caught up in that old game of hers.
Inappropriate talk shared with me.

Another Wedding

Two years later, Sam sent out invitations to his wedding. He also had to explain to his fiancé's parents about his father. These invitations include his parents as "Maureen and Alice." Again, Maureen appeared in the man's suit as Martin.

"Why didn't you come as Maureen?"

Again, she shrugged, "I thought it would be better this way." This time there were members of her extended family in attendance, her brother and cousins, stepmother uncles and aunts. Everyone kept pleasantries on the surface.

The End

In February 2018, Maureen contacted me asking to meet in the middle. She lived in Portland and I in the Seattle area. We had over the years met several times near Olympia, a two-hour drive for each of us. We agreed on a date and met on a rainy Tuesday at Shari's restaurant.

She was happy to have sold her house but also concerned that she would not be able to find a reasonable rental while she waited to have a house built. I was surprised to hear that she and her partner were going to buy this next house together. After recent conflicts between them, it seemed more logical to move on separately.

For the second time, she asked me to act as the executor of her estate should something happen to her. She was not in good health and had a long list of ailments. Her most recent complaint was heart palpitations.

I looked across the table at her and realized that she was stuck in the middle again. Neither female nor male. I addressed this with her.

"What are you doing? Who are you?"

She shrugged. "I'm tired of people staring at me. I'm tired of having to explain myself."

I wanted to ask if she regretted having the surgery, but she had already told me that what she regretted was losing the family. That brought up another regurgitated conversation about how she should keep in contact with the boys. To which she would respond that she tried but they did not respond. When I questioned them, they said the same thing. They would respond and make contact, but then after one conversation, she would not respond. I took a sip of water and pushed those thoughts away.

"Anyway," she said, "I want you to take care of everything. Everything goes to the boys and ..."

"Do you have a will?"

"Yes, of course."

On May 9, 2019, Maureen died from a massive heart attack. I was contacted by her partner, then I called and informed the boys, Maureen's brother and stepmother. Together the boys and I made arrangements to go and pack up and dispose of Maureen's things.

There was no will. Maureen had moved into this home the previous year and never fully unpacked. She did all her banking and bill paying online. We had no passwords, no way to access any of her accounts.

We had talked since the divorce of how we would name each other as executors and leave everything to the boys. She had not followed through. Her partner was joint tenant on the house, so she would take the house and wanted nothing more.

Prior to our visit, I made an appointment with a probate attorney. We would arrive the day before that meeting and try to locate a will. Having none, we met with the attorney and signed papers naming me as the Executor and the boys as the only heirs.

We sorted through what was Maureen's. One boy would say that the bin of scuba gear was valuable; another would check prices on eBay and call it trash. So, we went through what there was. There were two identical jackets hanging in the closet that must have been purchased as gifts for Arlo and Max but never delivered. They tried them on and took them home. Working from the division of assets in our divorce agreement and the credit cards in Maureen's wallet, I was able to ascertain her assets; thankfully there were no debts and closed the estate dividing the money among the four boys.

At the funeral home, the four boys and I stood vigil and said our own goodbyes. I kissed her forehead and wished her peace, something I thought she had been unable to find in life.

In the end we want to come out even. I called one of the credit card companies and identifying myself as the executor was able to get a current balance.

"But wait," the customer service agent said, "there is a credit balance in rewards." There was a nine cent difference to which she said, "We'll handle that."

With her death the boys lost the opportunity to ever reconnect with their dad. Each expressed this pain with me.

Sadly, Maureen missed the birth of her grandson six weeks later.

Alice In GenderLand

190

Q&A With the Author

Q: The money. Everyone wants to know about the money spent on the surgeries.

A: The money came out of our joint account. But in the years before the surgery was scheduled Martin was making plans, secret plans, his plans. He was not sharing this plan with me, his wife, his partner. As it played out, this became understood. In one year, he worked as a contractor and because of his expertise in the semiconductor sector, he could pull in a salary over two hundred thousand. I brought in another half of that, and he set aside one hundred thousand dollars. I suggested we invest in a vacation property, something rural but within two hours' drive of home. He went along with this plan and even took a weekend trip to explore this option with me. He never said what he planned, but as he approached the subject, I began to see. The cost of the surgeries was not as outrageous as one might consider. Insurance plans wouldn't cover the costs as it was considered elective surgery, the doctors worked to make them affordable. The sexual reassignment surgery was under forty thousand, the facial feminization surgery was about twenty-five thousand, and the vocal cord surgery was another ten thousand. Add to that the cost of travel and hotel stays, the one hundred thousand covered it all.

The next question is usually how I felt about him spending your money for that. Long ago I resolved that if this would make him happy, truly happy, no more depression, no more moodiness, make him be a fully involved human, then spare no expense and do it.

Q: Did it resolve all the issues?

A: Sadly, it did not. She was neither a happy nor fully integrated person; she was still Martin but now with a female body. Instead of pursing a heterosexual relationship which is what she said she wanted, she chose a relationship with another woman.

Q: Did she regret the transition:

A: We talked about this when we met and while she regretted that she had not worked harder to keep our family together, she did not regret the gender change. We did discuss her lack of success in being recognized as female. She was unnerved if anyone looked at her askance as if to question her womanhood. She felt that the lack of a higher pitched voice was her undoing. She reverted to a raspy whisper ala Marilyn Monroe which made her inaudible.

Q: Why did you write this book? Aren't you concerned about what your privacy?

A: I remember how alone I felt when this started. I didn't know anyone who had been through it and one thing you want is to understand what lies ahead. I wrote this for anyone who may be dealing with a loved one who is gender dysphoric – and I have shared my story many times with people. My sons are fully aware of this and have no qualms about the book.

Q: What is your takeaway from this experience?

A: First it is that I know that I acted the way I would want my partner to treat me if this was me. Second, that my view was opened to know and embrace trans people. Finally, to learn over and over again that fear sets us on the wrong path – and as I quoted Ted Lasso – "Be curious, not judgmental."

Acknowledgements

I would never have been able to work through these pages without the support of my writing groups and my beta readers. Thank you to:

Judy Duncan
Jon Eekhoff
Joan Enoch MD
Ruth Marcus
Carol Marting
Melee McGuire
Linda B. Myers
Rebecca Redshaw
Carol Rich
Donna Whichello

Made in the USA
Columbia, SC
29 January 2023